Annette LeMay Burke

FAUXLIAGE

Disguised Cell Phone Towers of the American West

Daylight

Cofounders: Taj Forer and Michael Itkoff
Creative Director: Ursula Damm
Copy Editor: Gabrielle Fastman

© 2020 Daylight Community Arts Foundation

Photographs © 2020 by Annette LeMay Burke

Foreword © 2020 by Ann M. Jastrab
What's Up with That Tree? © 2020 by Annette LeMay Burke

All rights reserved.

ISBN: 978-1-942084-98-3

Printed by OFSET YAPIMEVİ, Turkey

Daylight Books
E-mail: info@daylightbooks.org
Web: www.daylightbooks.org

FOREWORD by Ann M. Jastrab

Years ago, I met Annette LeMay Burke when her project *Fauxliage* was in its infancy. I wrote a short review of the work and declared that I wanted the series to be a book, and, finally, my dream has come true. I am honored that she asked me to write the foreword for this monograph. Honored and also strangely saddened because does this mean her search is over? The project complete? I lean back and already begin thinking about a second edition or the Second Coming, which may sound blasphemous, but once you see some of the images in this book, you will wonder at what lengths the cell phone companies will go to for the greatest coverage.

The first time I saw this collection of images, I realized Annette had been making a document. Initially what I saw were picturesque landscapes. But, wait, what was happening in these views? Something was amiss. In these beautifully composed scenes, there were giant saguaro cacti, palm trees reflected in crystal clear pools, and a towering pine tree in a barren desert. And therein lay the problem: What was a pine tree doing in the middle of the Mojave Desert with not even a tuft of grass to be seen nearby? I looked a little closer. These weren't real live trees at all. These were what we called "Frankenpines" in upstate New York where I grew up: cell phone towers disguised as fake trees. Usually the trees blend in with the surrounding foliage. In Annette LeMay Burke's *Fauxliage* this was not always the case. I couldn't help but laugh and look again, and then again, taking my hat off to the brilliant title as well. It became almost like a game of "Where's Waldo?" in some images. The trees looked part of the landscape: a tall palm overlooking a line of U-Haul trucks, or a eucalyptus just hanging out next to the side of the road. Other times, they were so cleverly hidden, I gasped. The Holy Trinity at the local church is really three cell phone towers? I'm not religious, but this might be a form of blasphemy. Or genius, as the cell phone companies are paying the church good money to plant those there. But sometimes the trees stood out starkly in their "native" environments; there is one image of what looks like a bright green plastic hula skirt crudely covering a tower buried in an oak forest. Who designed that one? The audacity of the engineers of these towers surprises.

These man-made creations, big in our landscapes, both urban and rural, are hidden in Annette's photographs, which are, by the way, beautifully rendered. Sometimes with the raking light of dusk in the desert bathing the towers with that incredible color that comes on with silence. Other times with the pure light of dawn before the wind has picked up and the air is stirred. Then there are the ones that are lit with the stark noon light where you feel the heat of the concrete city around you and you look up at the tree that offers no shade...only to realize it isn't a tree at all.

Annette has created something even better than I could have imagined. She has made an object, and as a book collector, I am obsessed with the photography book as an object and a piece of art. Yes, Annette has produced an object that I can pick up and look at repeatedly and have a good chuckle and a deep sigh, thinking of the things humankind has done right and done wrong. I find myself now driving around California and looking for these disguised towers, in all their many forms. What would the Bechers have done with this subject? There is too much variety, too much wildness to control here. I imagine they might have walked away. But not Annette.

It's a smart project, this one. *Fauxliage* presents a landscape like no other.

Ann M. Jastrab is currently the executive director of the Center for Photographic Art (CPA) in Carmel, California.

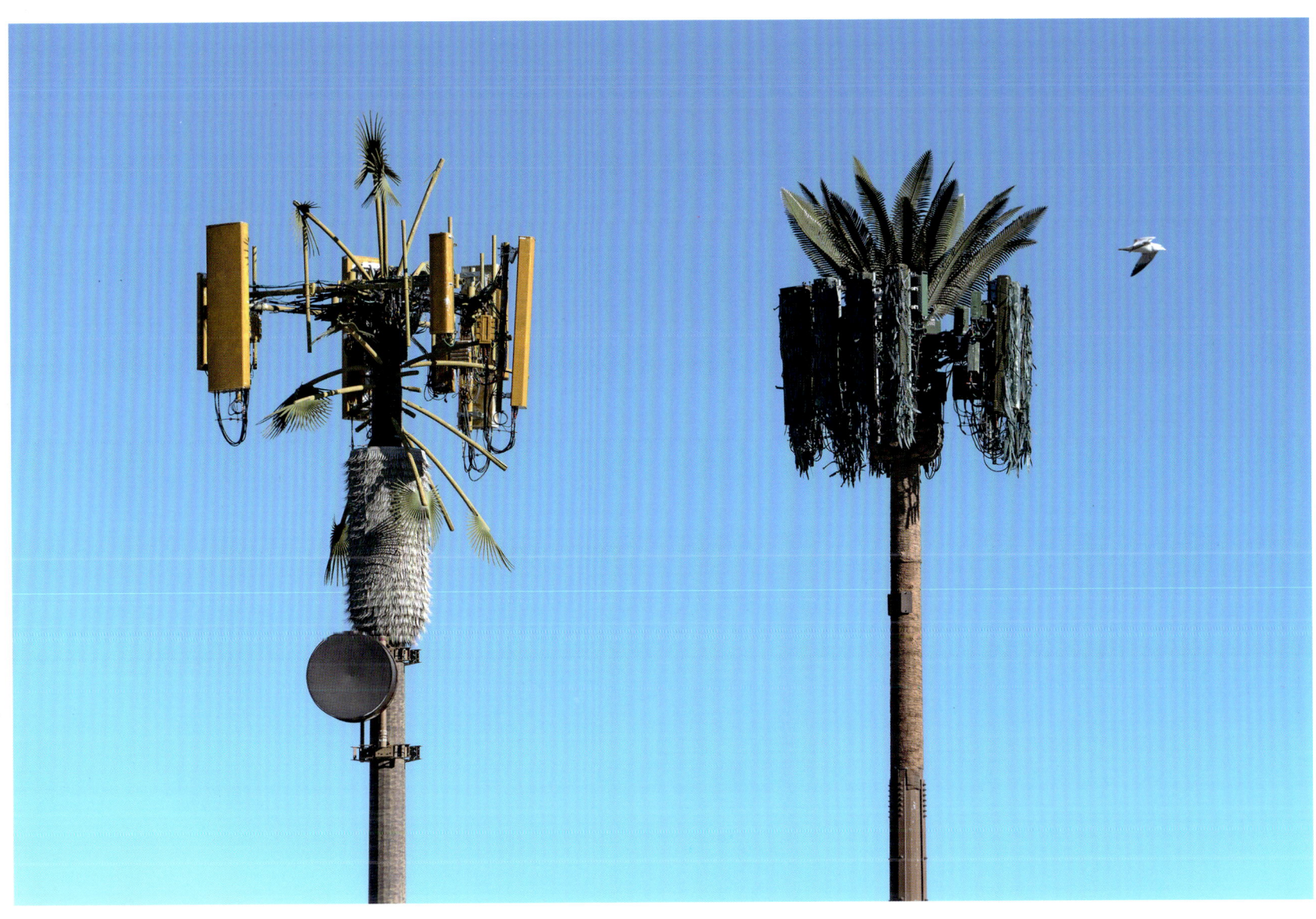

Twin Palms, Mecca, CA – 2019

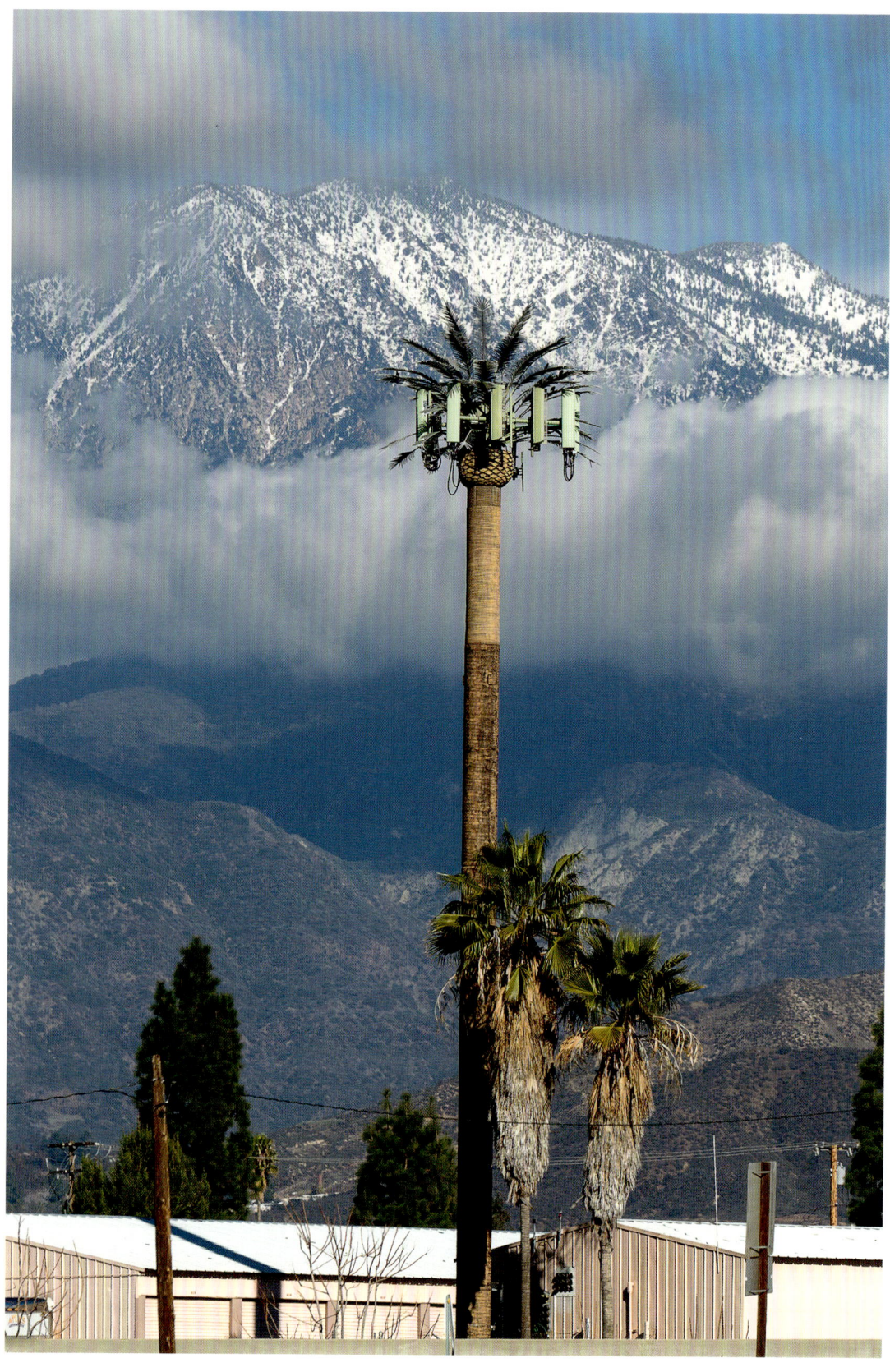

Palm in Winter, Calimesa, CA – 2017

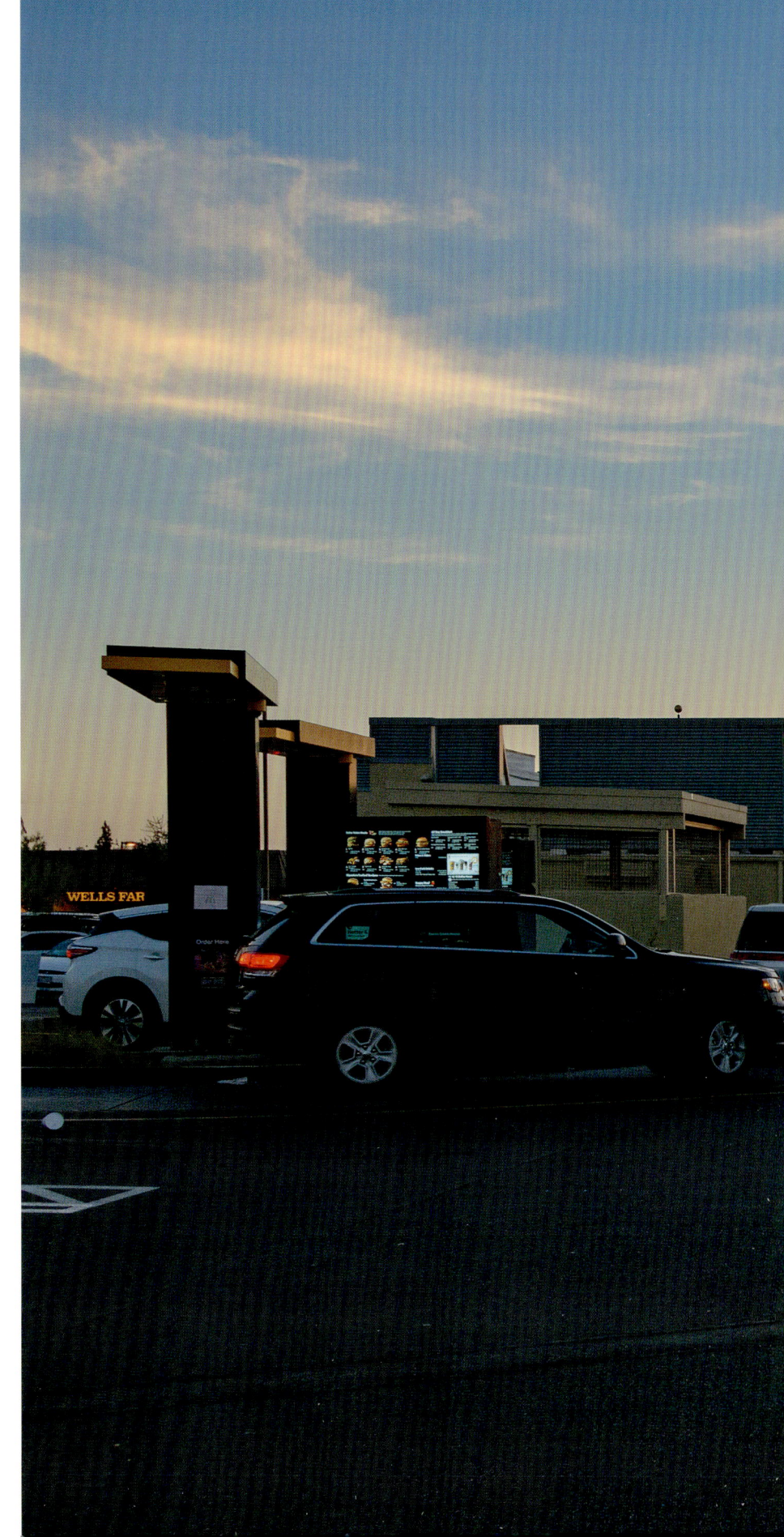

Drive-Thru, La Mesa, CA – 2018

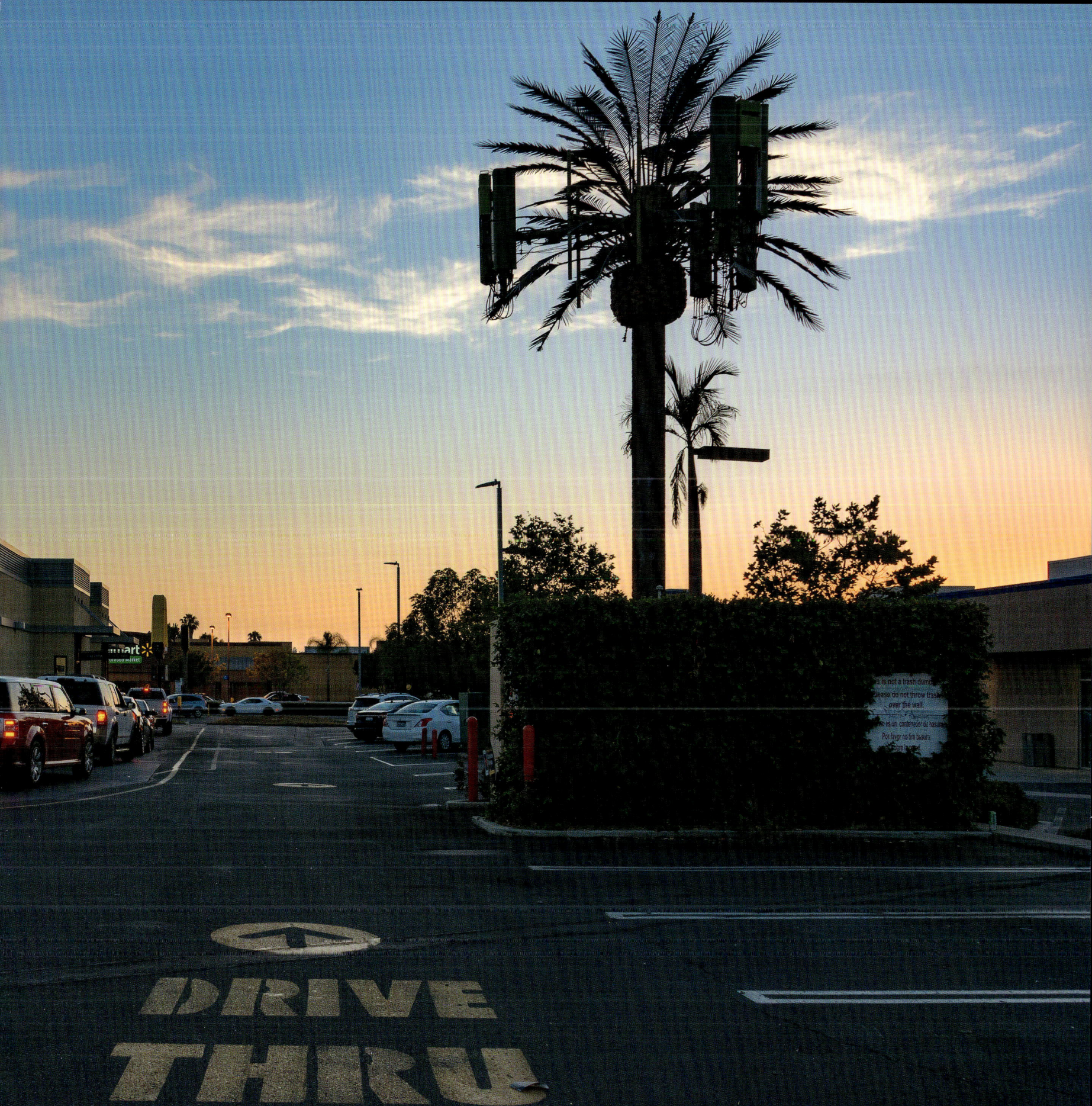

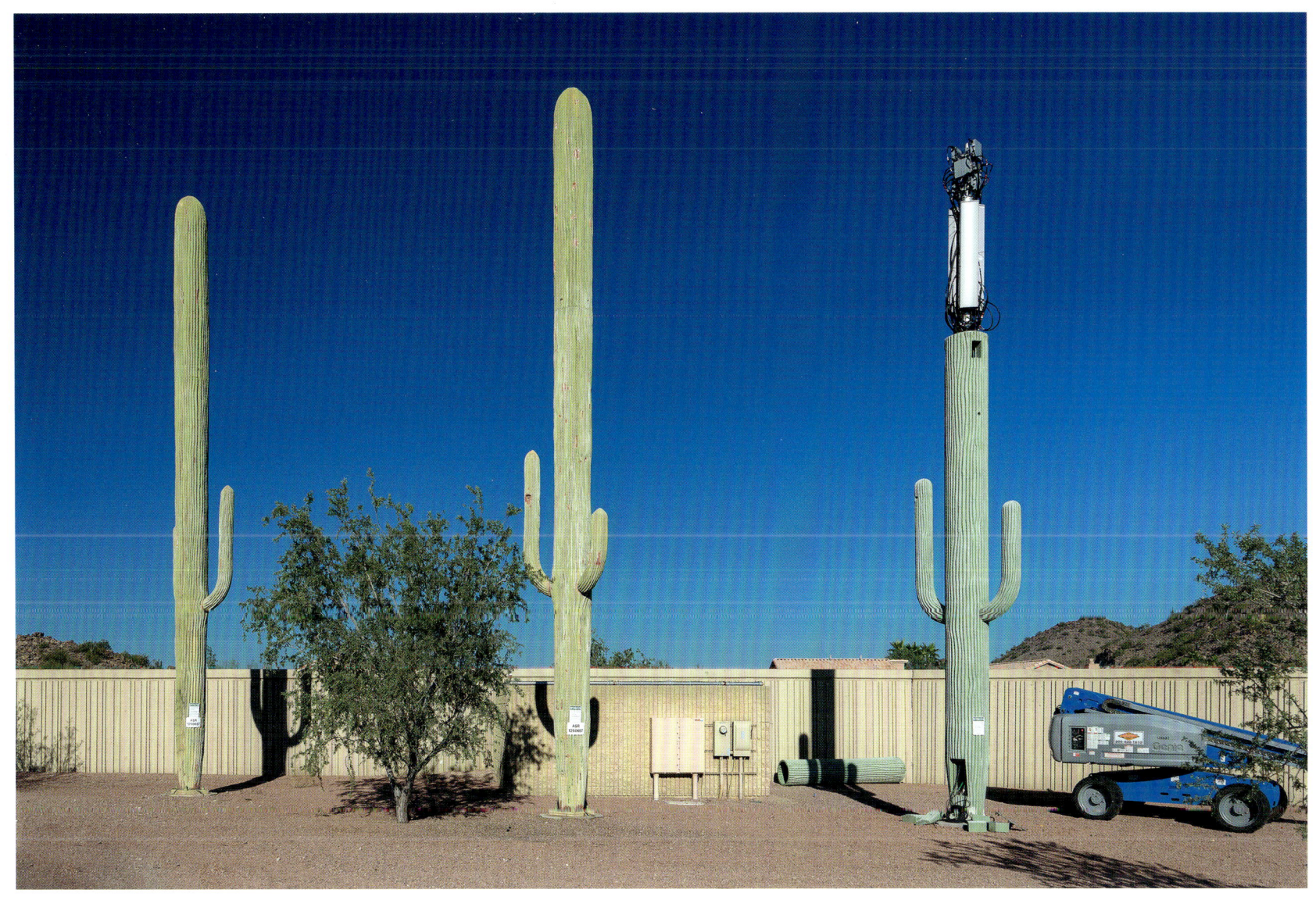

Three Saguaros, Phoenix, AZ – 2016

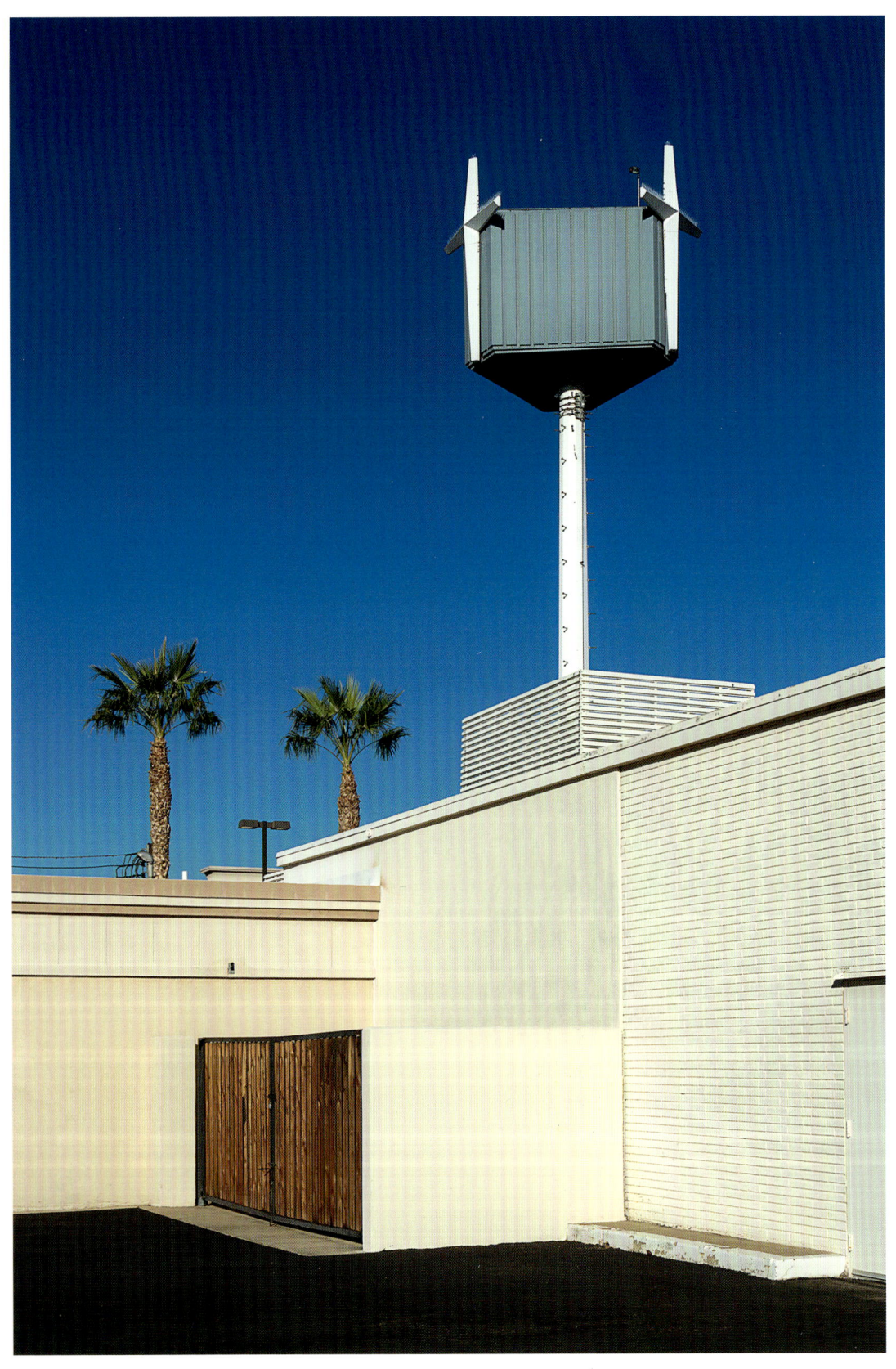

Calvary Megachurch, Phoenix, AZ – 2016

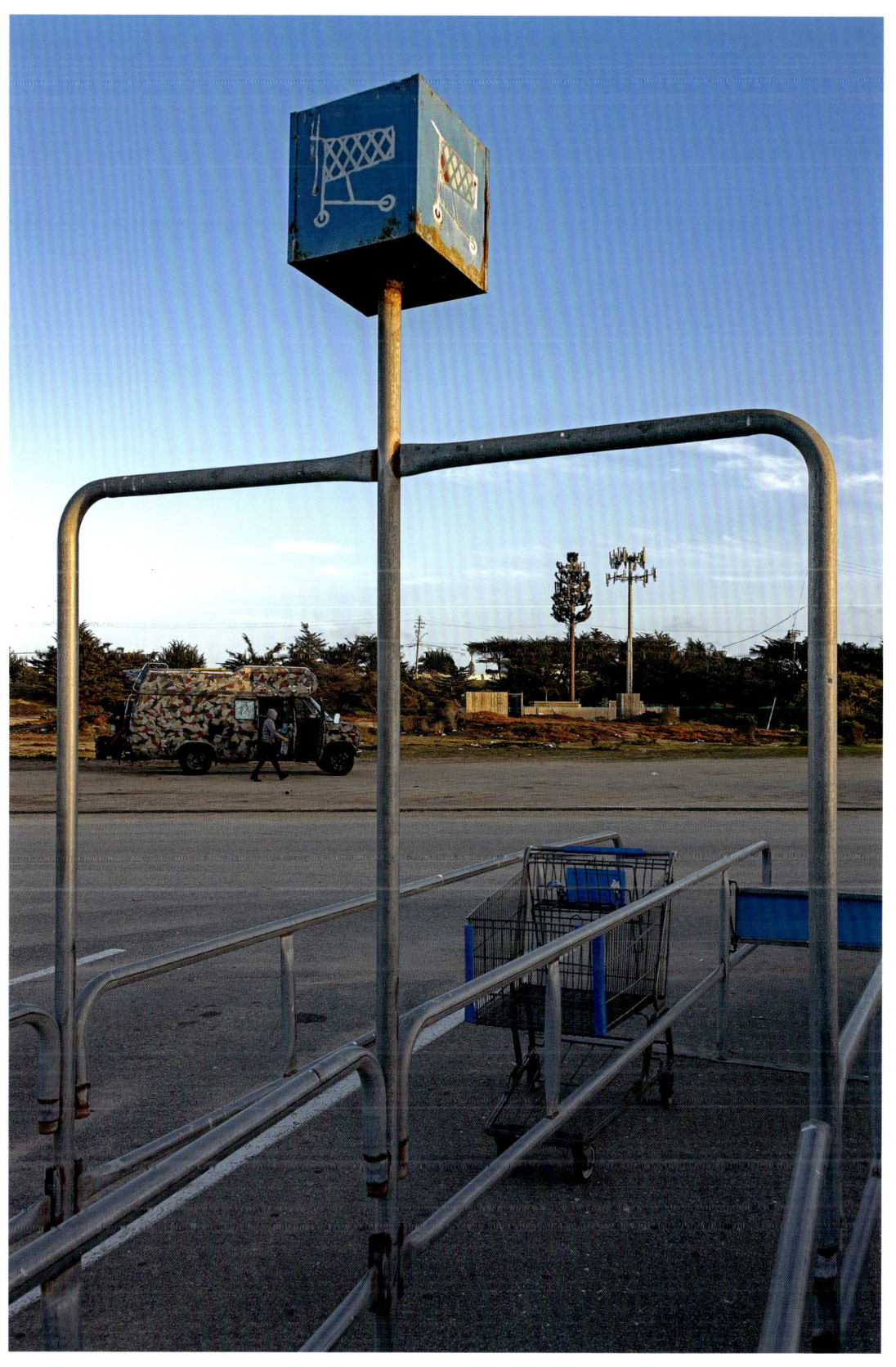

Checked Out, Marina, CA – 2020

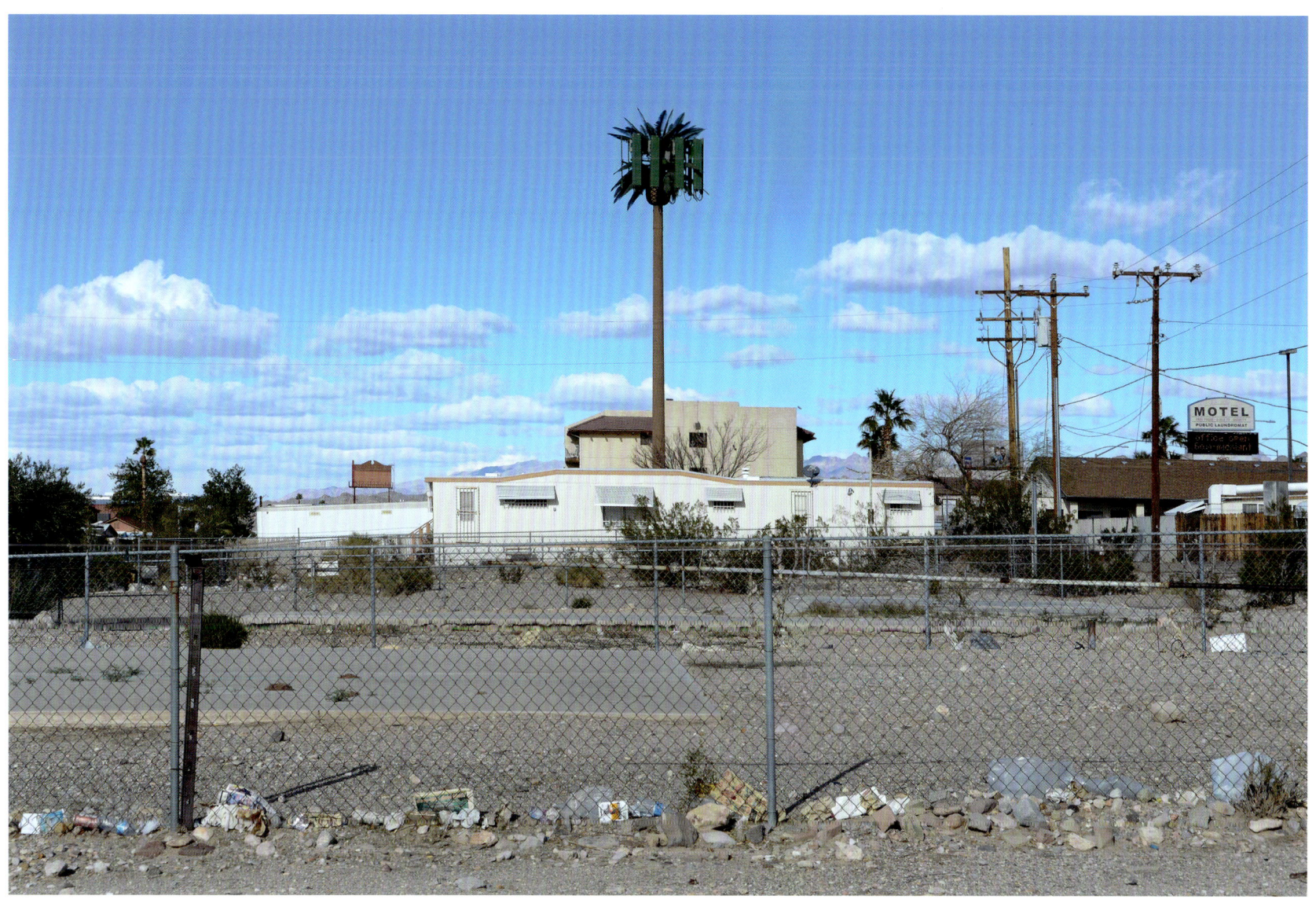

Ungentrified, Bullhead City, AZ – 2018

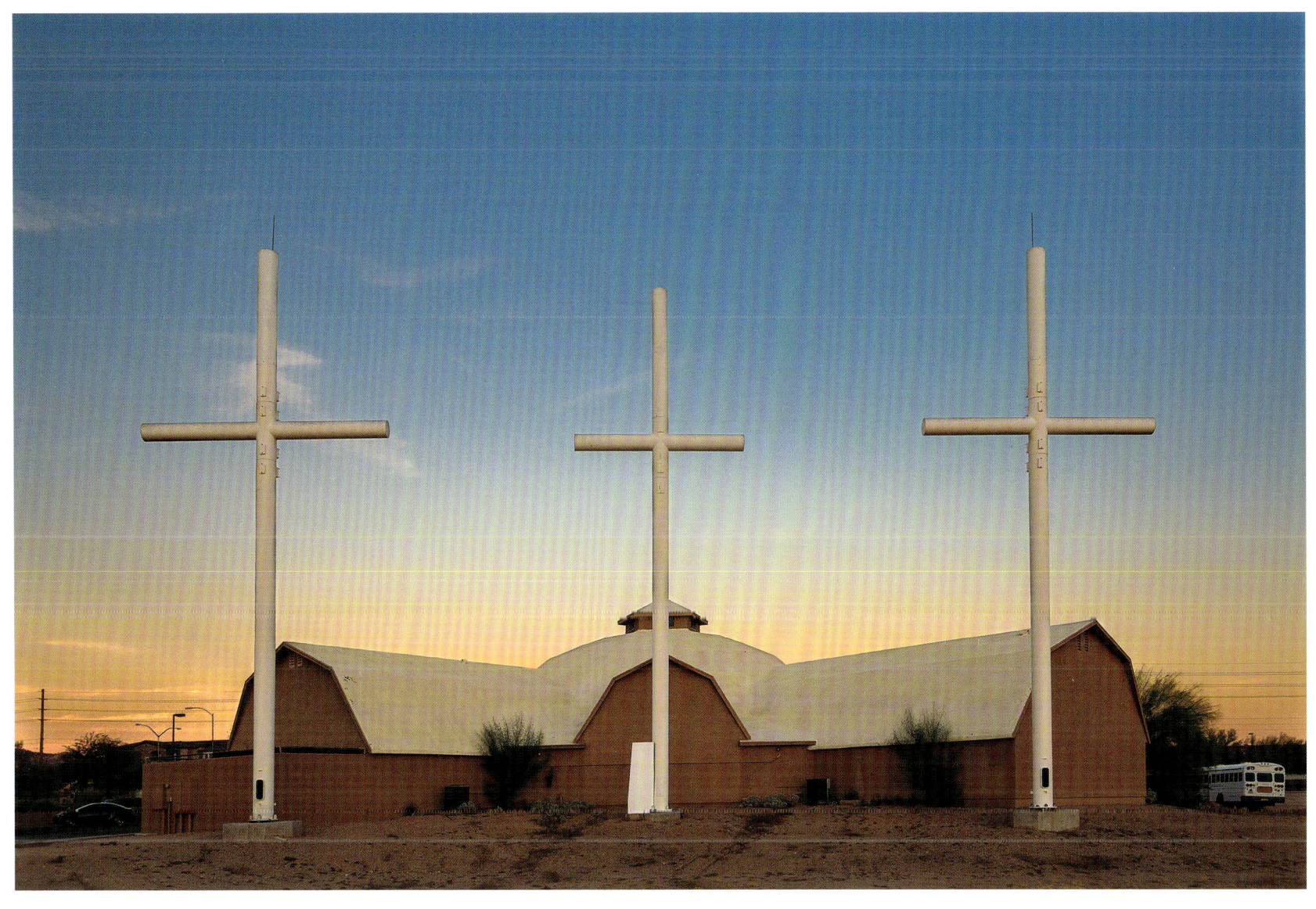

The Middle Cross, Mesa, AZ – 2016

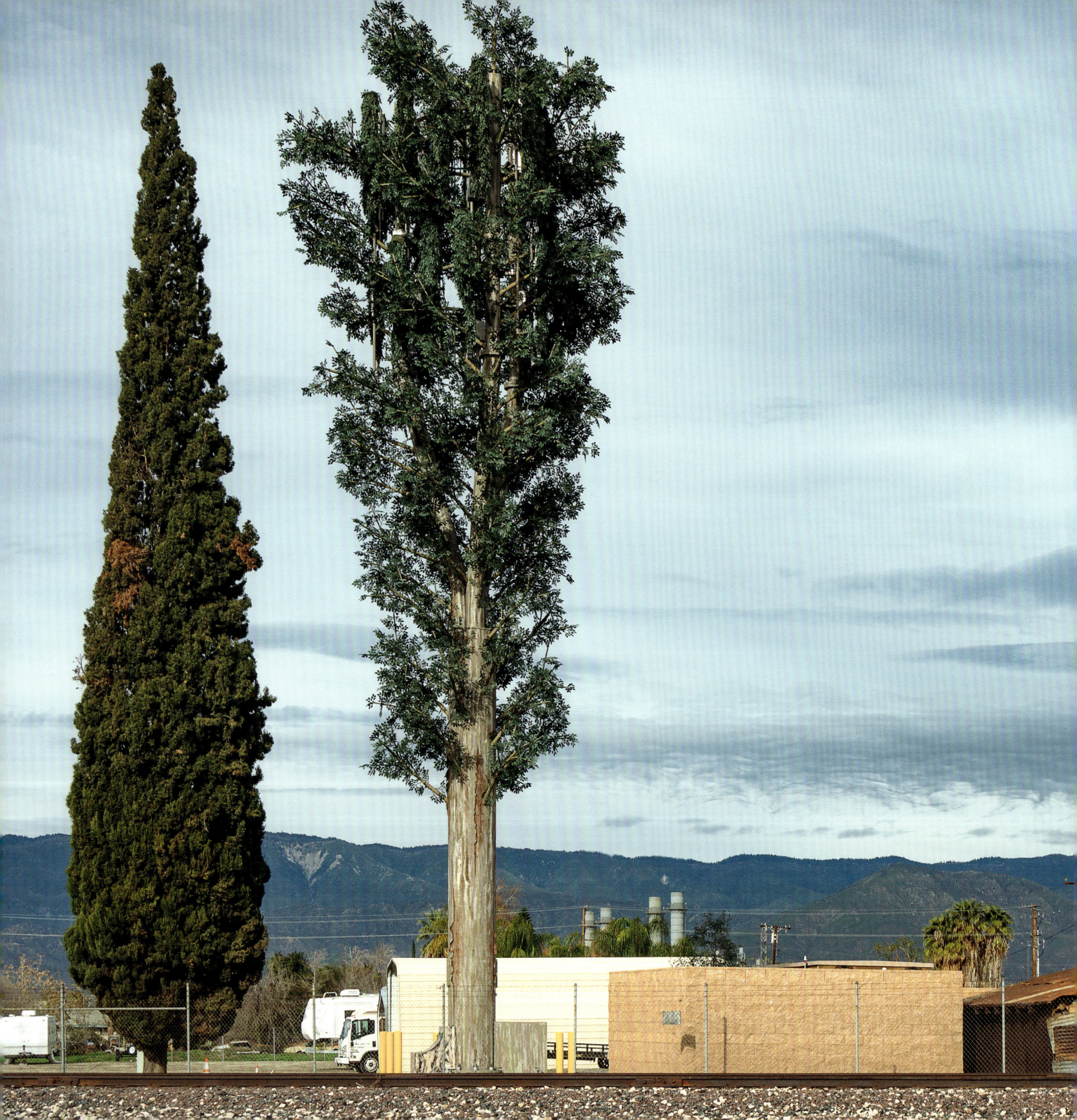

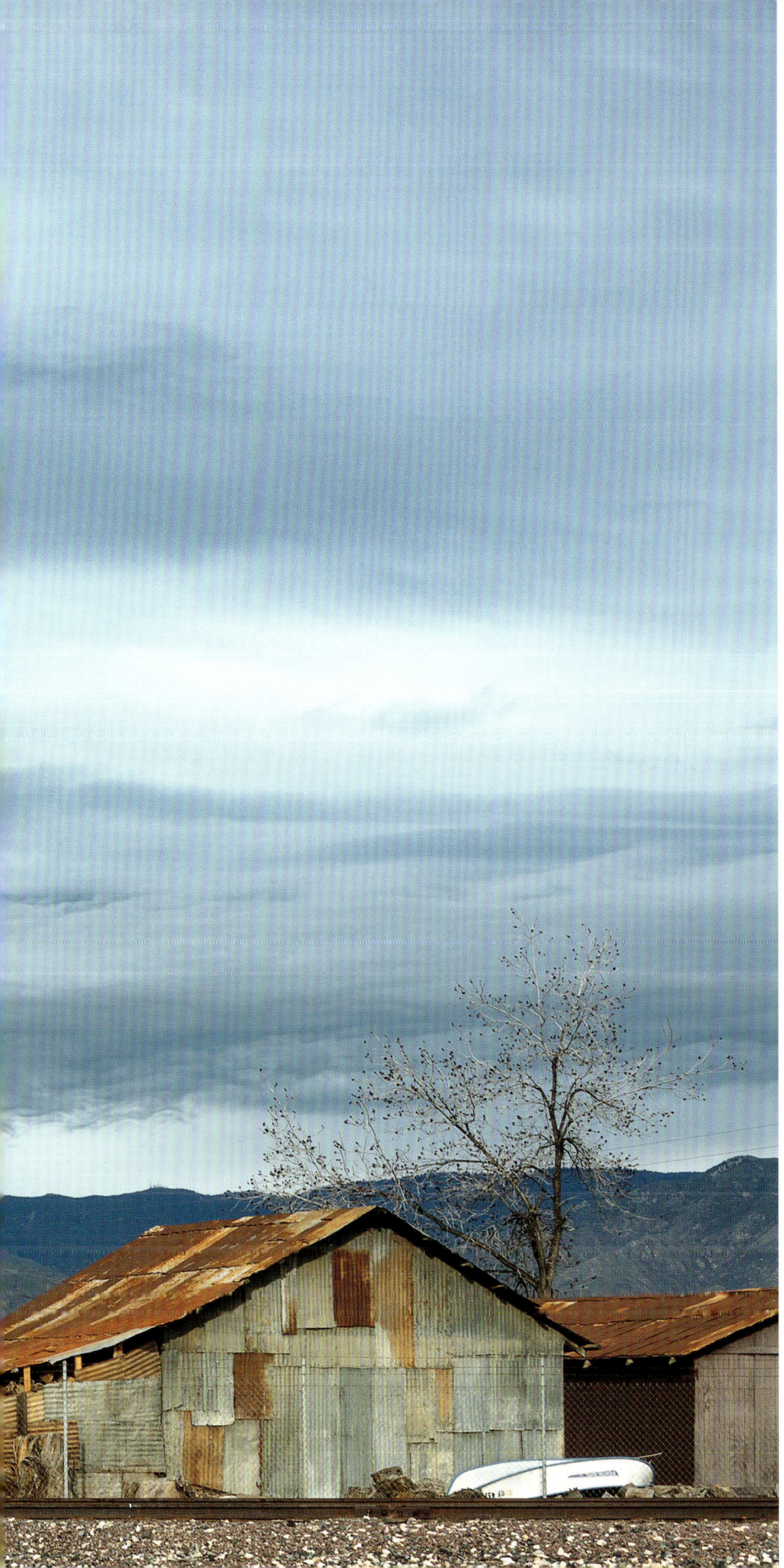

Eucalyptus, San Bernardino, CA – 2017

23

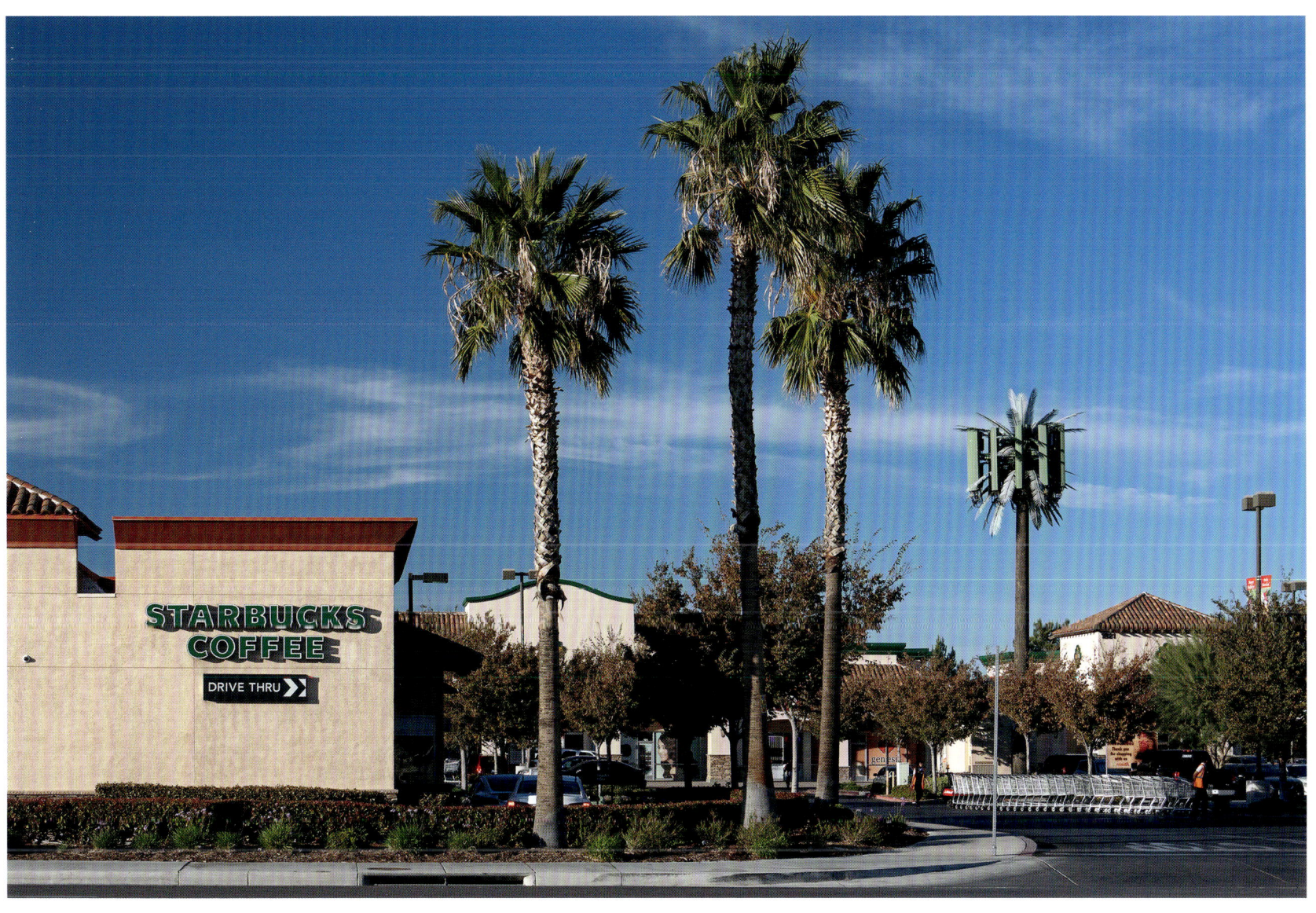

Signal Boost, Lancaster, CA – 2019

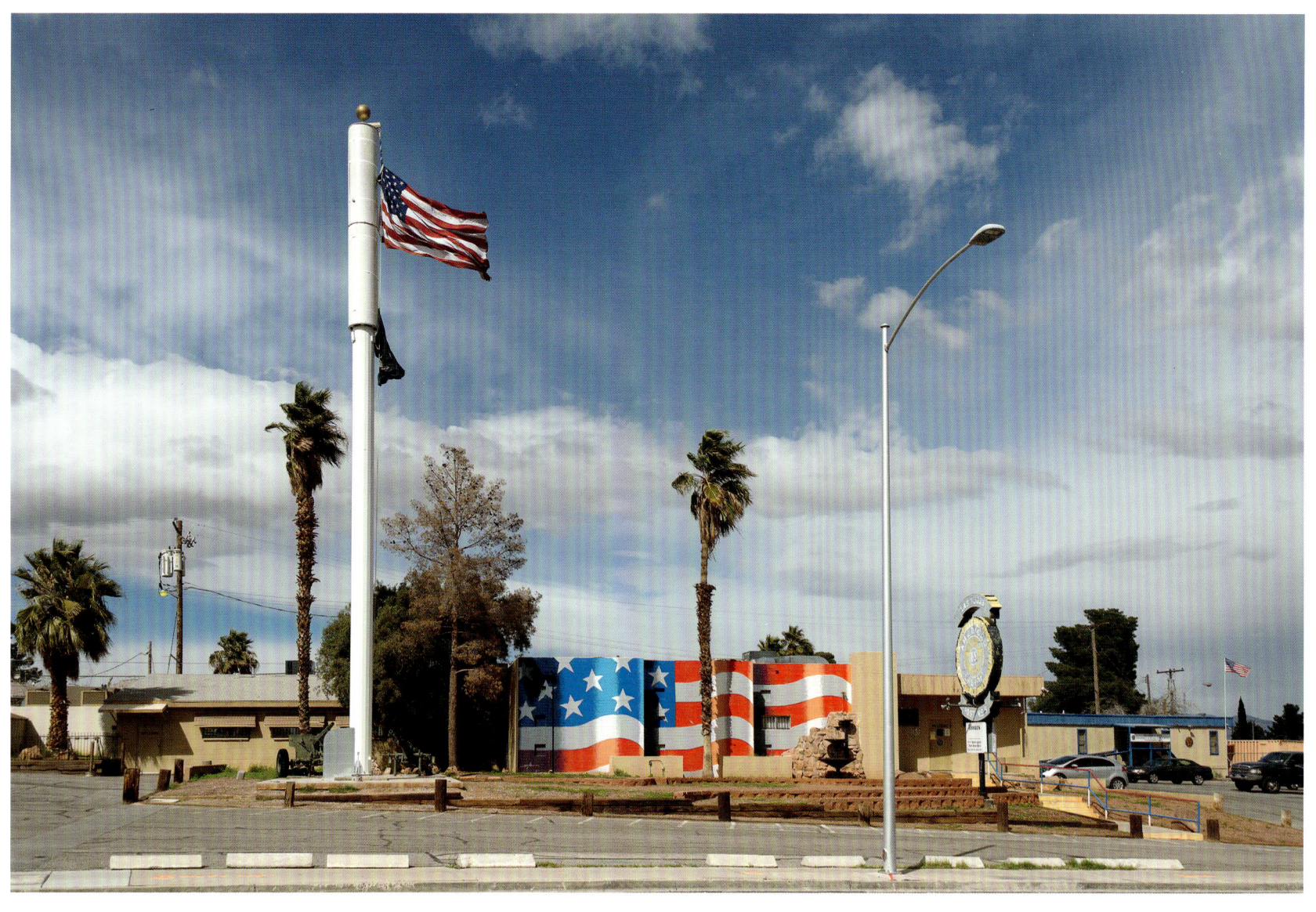

American Legion Flags, Las Vegas, NV – 2019

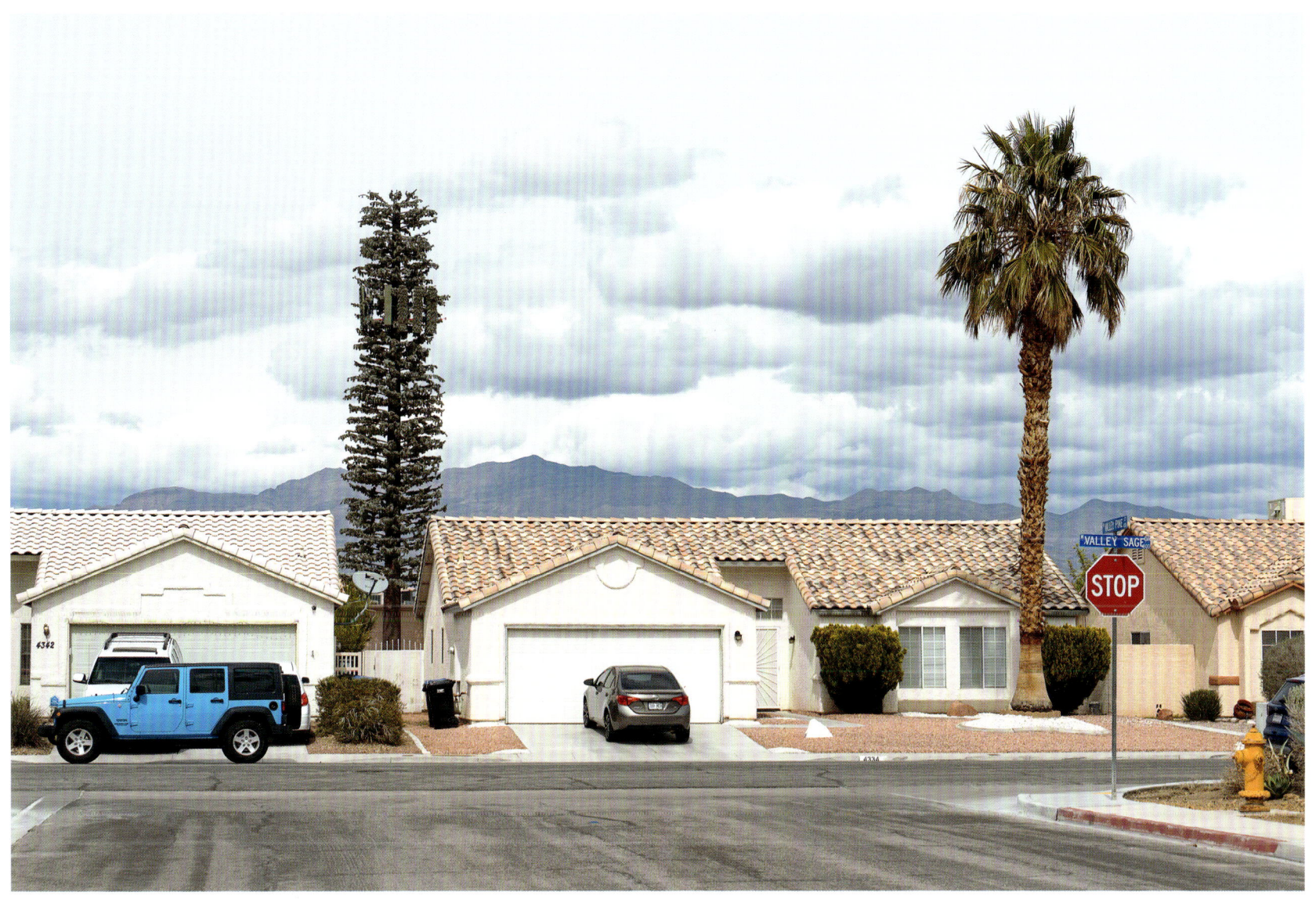

Suburban Dreams, Las Vegas, NV – 2019

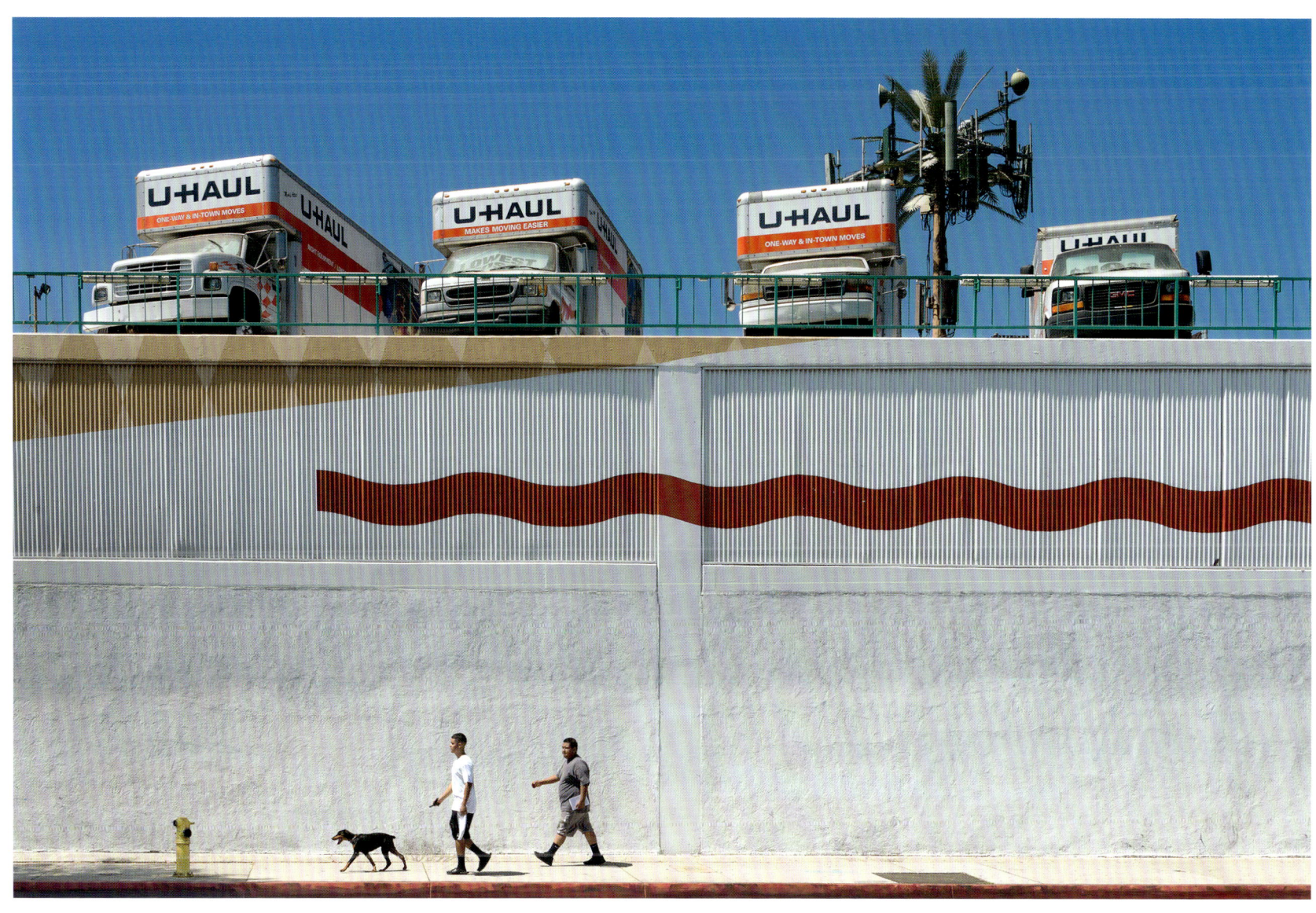

Oversee, East Los Angeles, CA – 2016

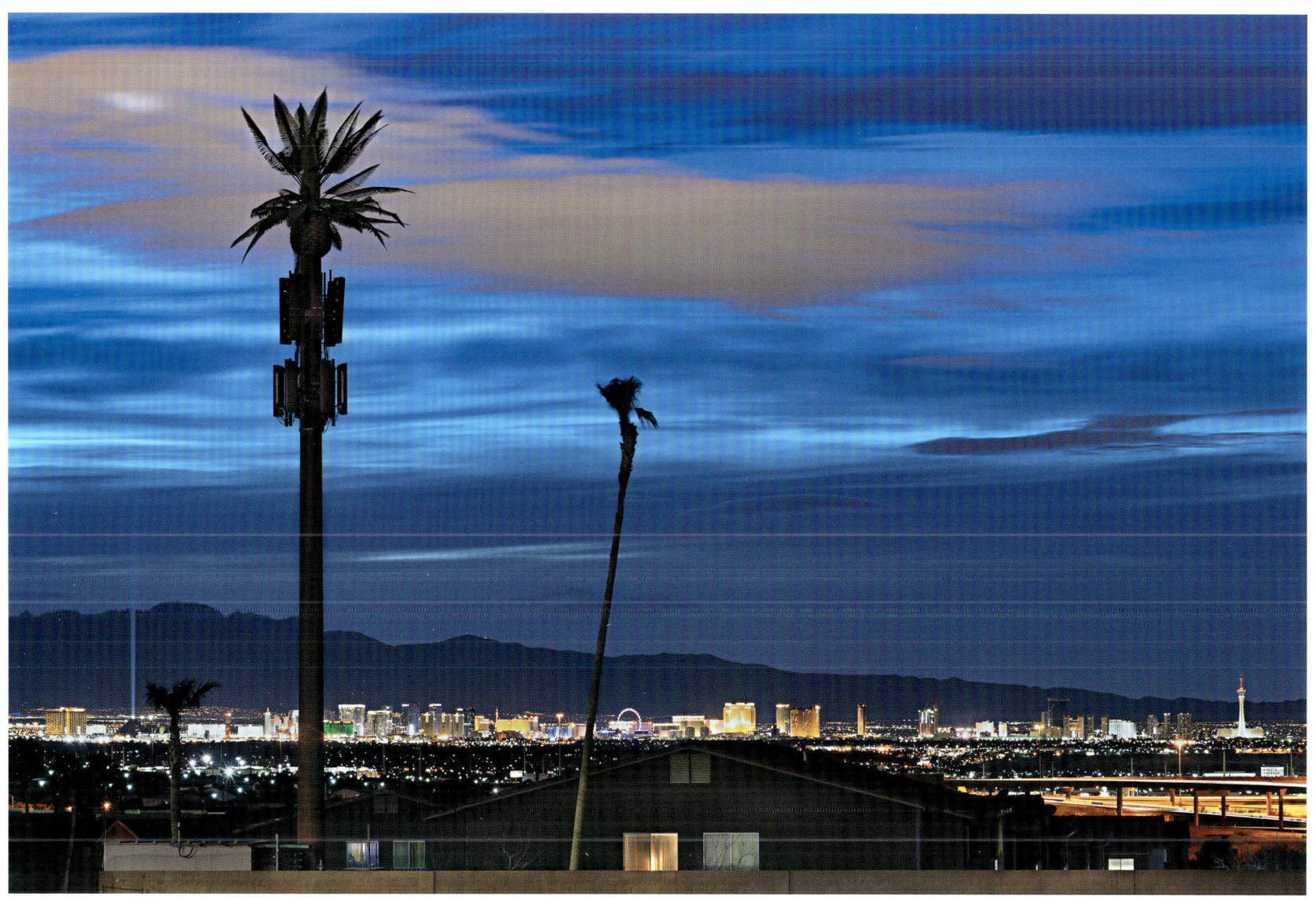

Vegas Strip, Henderson, NV – 2019

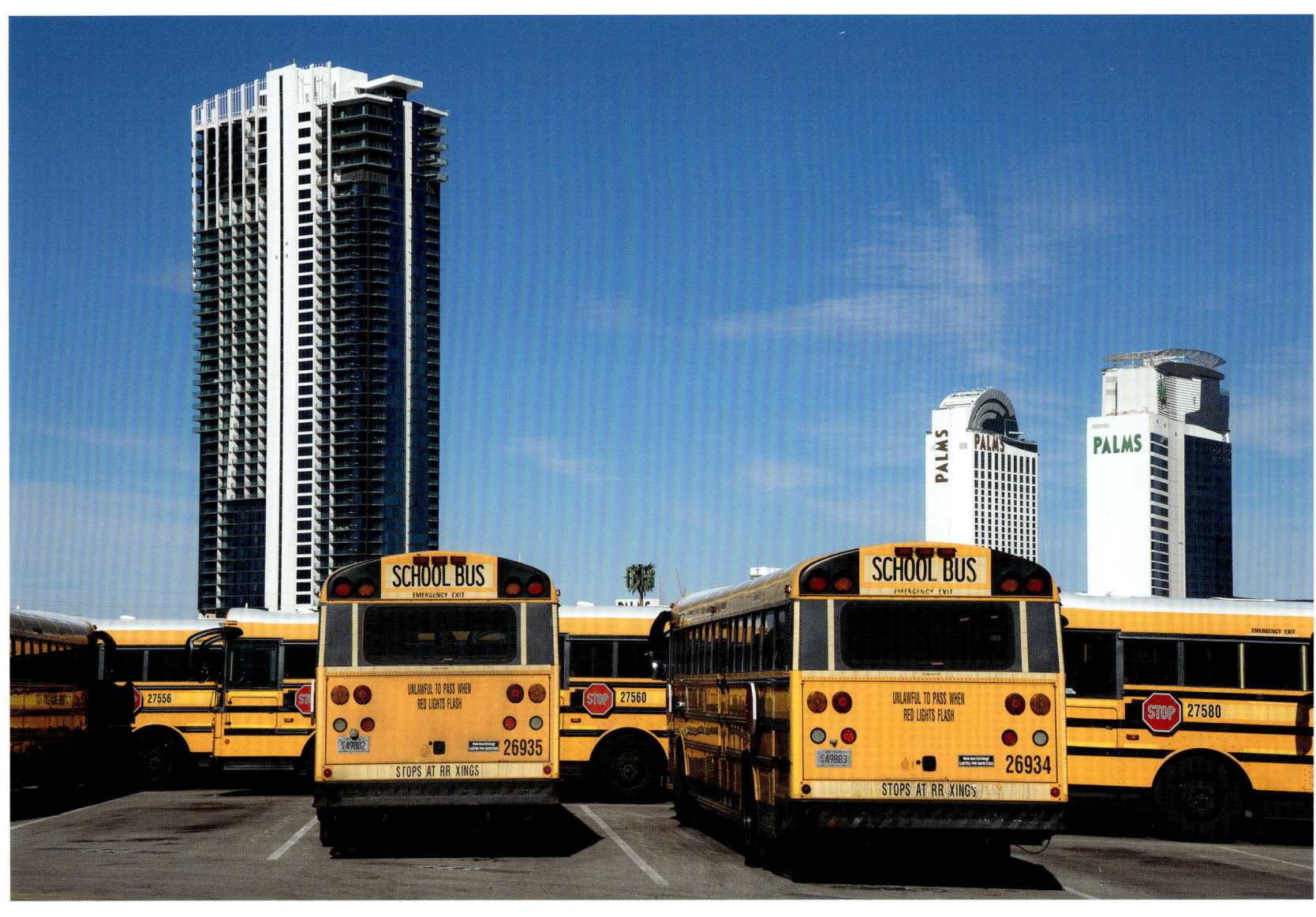

Between the Buses, Las Vegas, NV – 2019

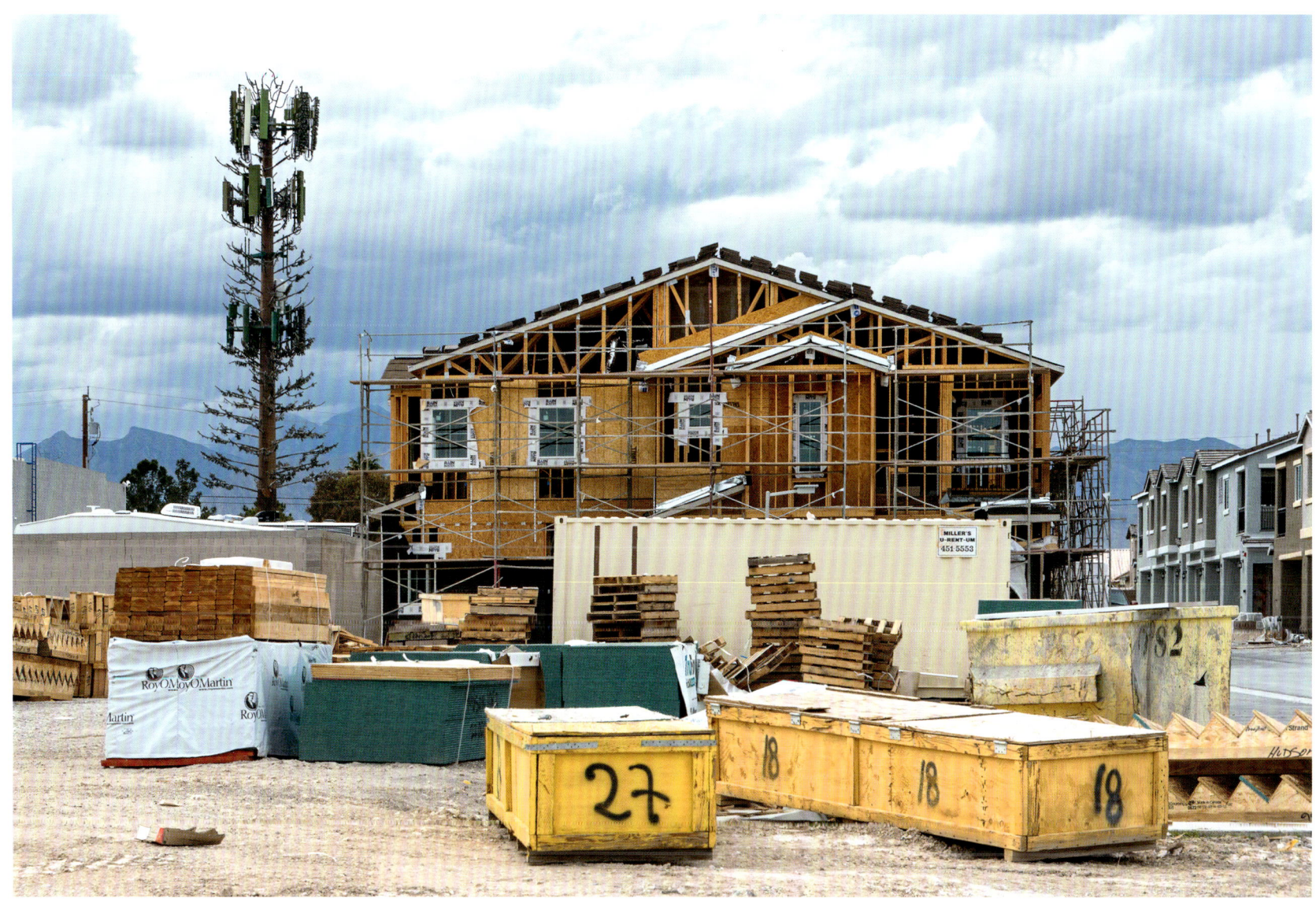

Move-In Condition, Las Vegas, NV – 2019

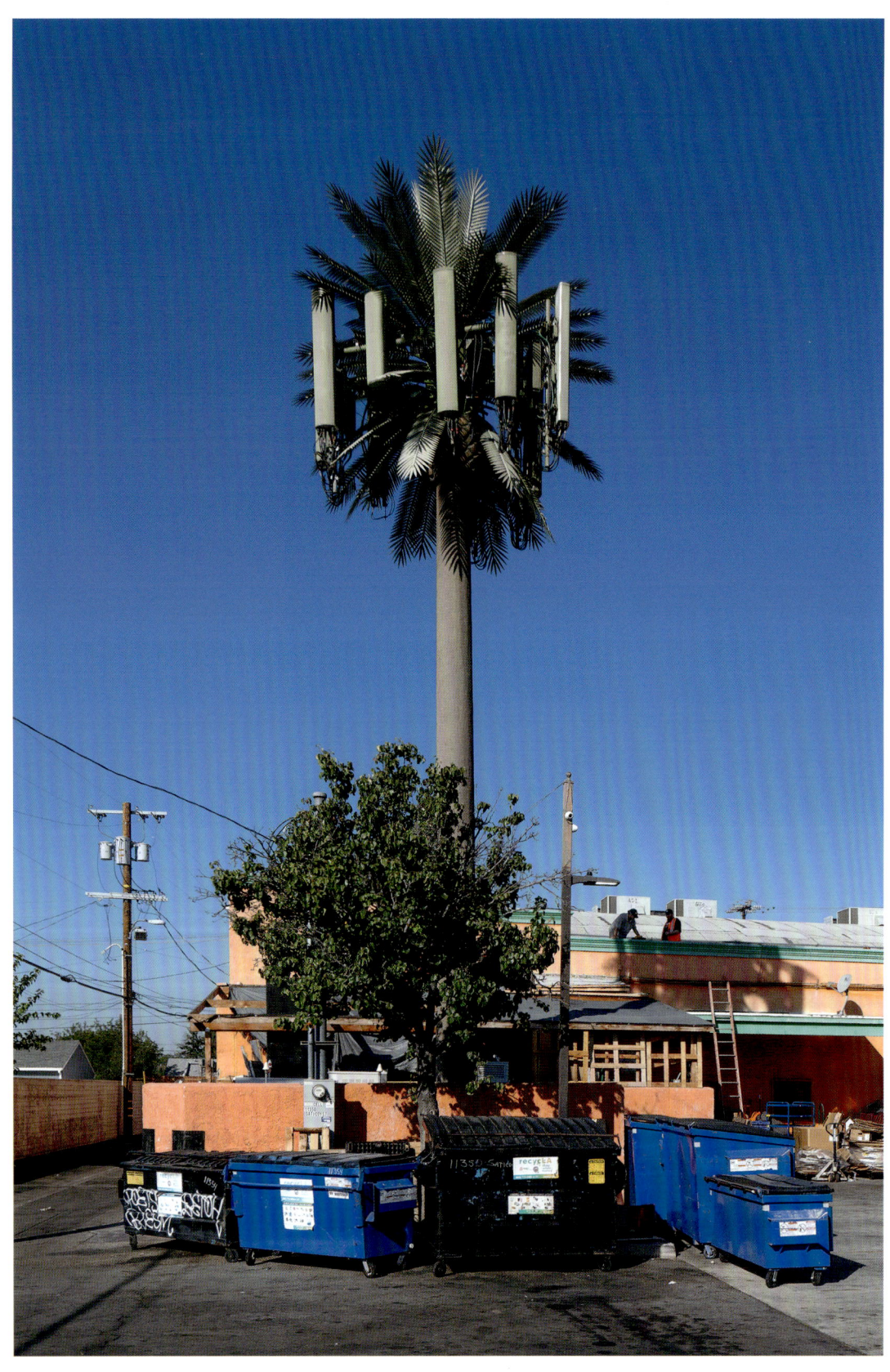

Dumpster Centerpiece, Sun Valley, CA – 2019

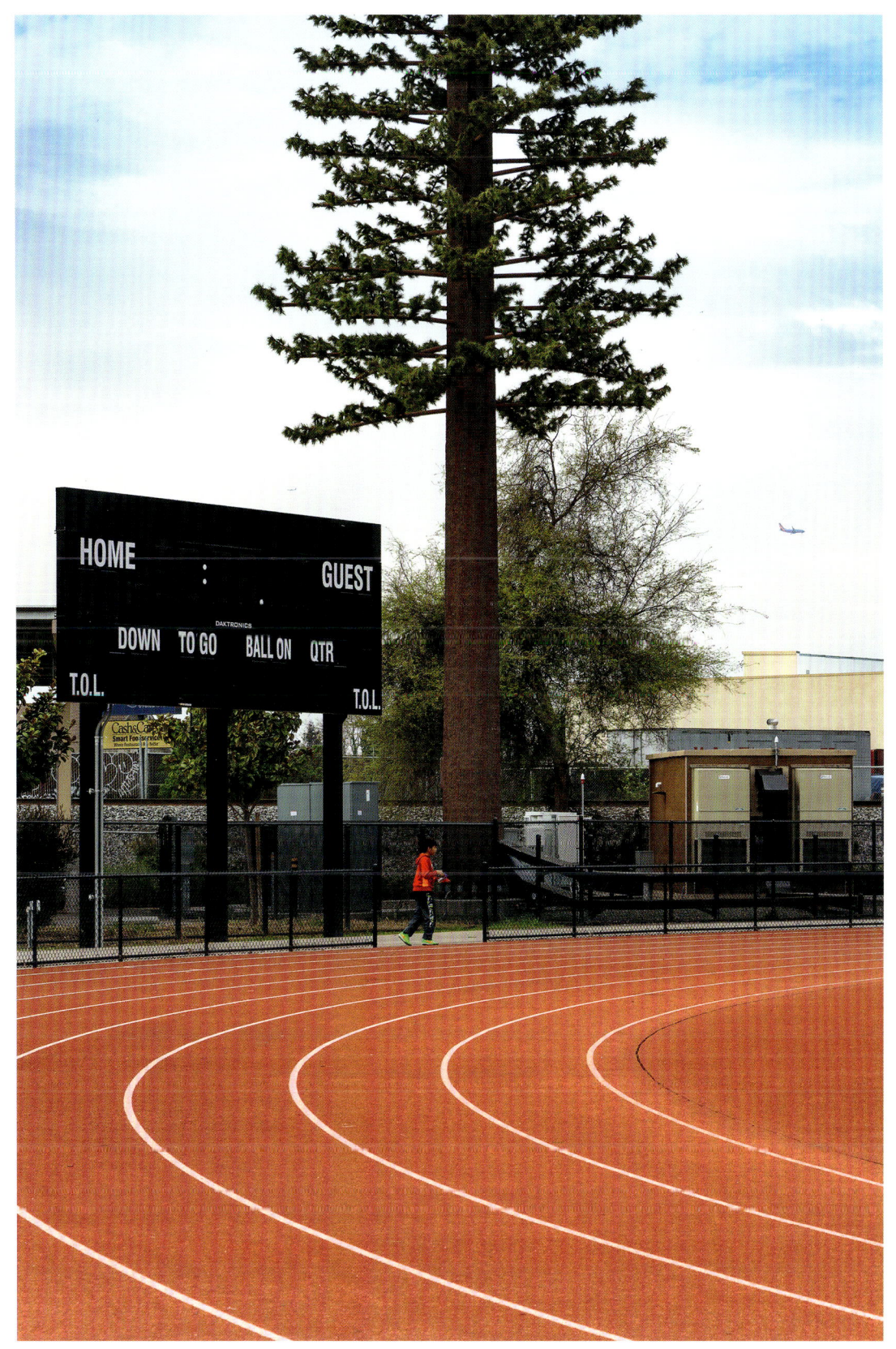

High School Track, San Lorenzo, CA – 2017

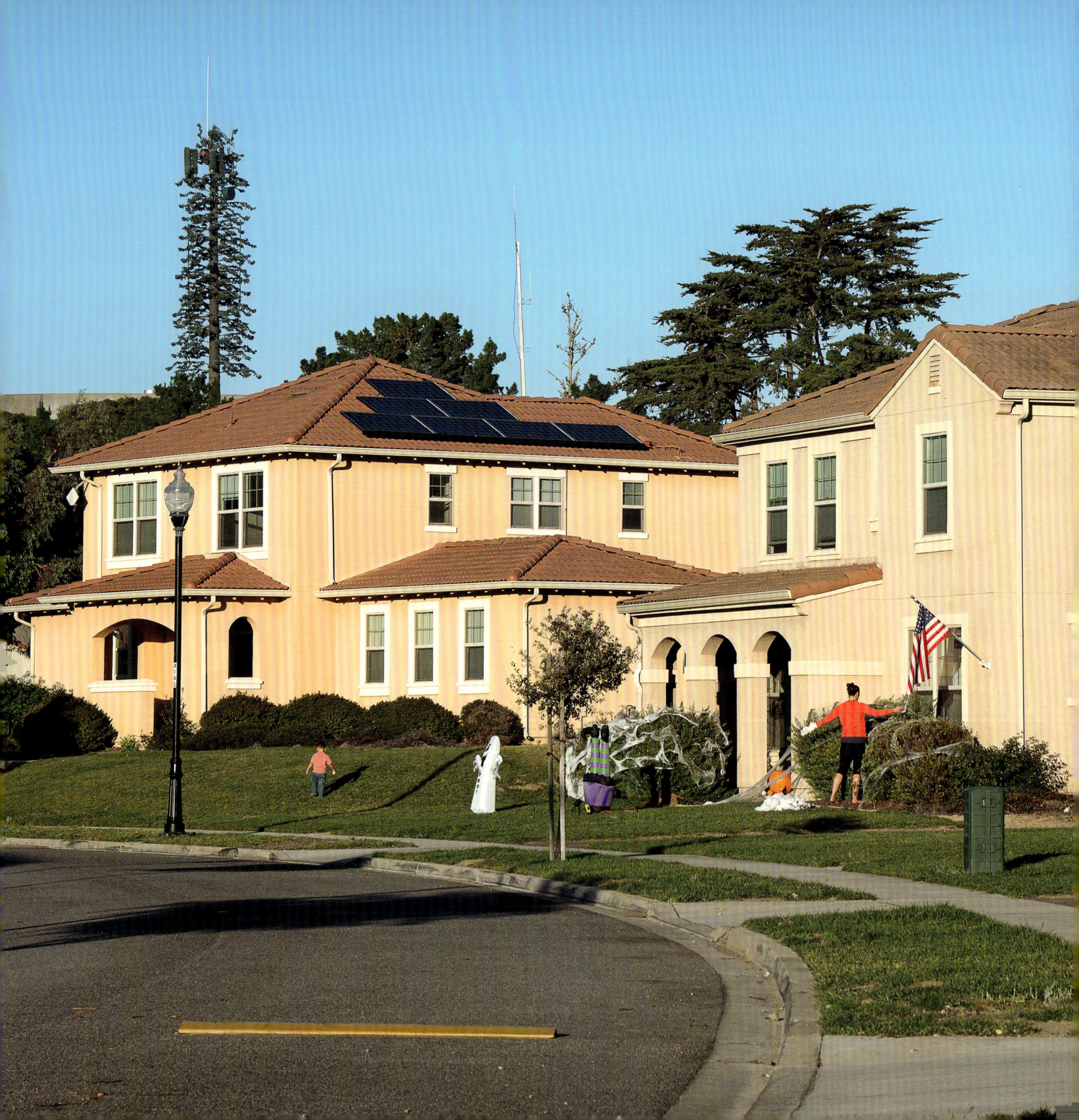

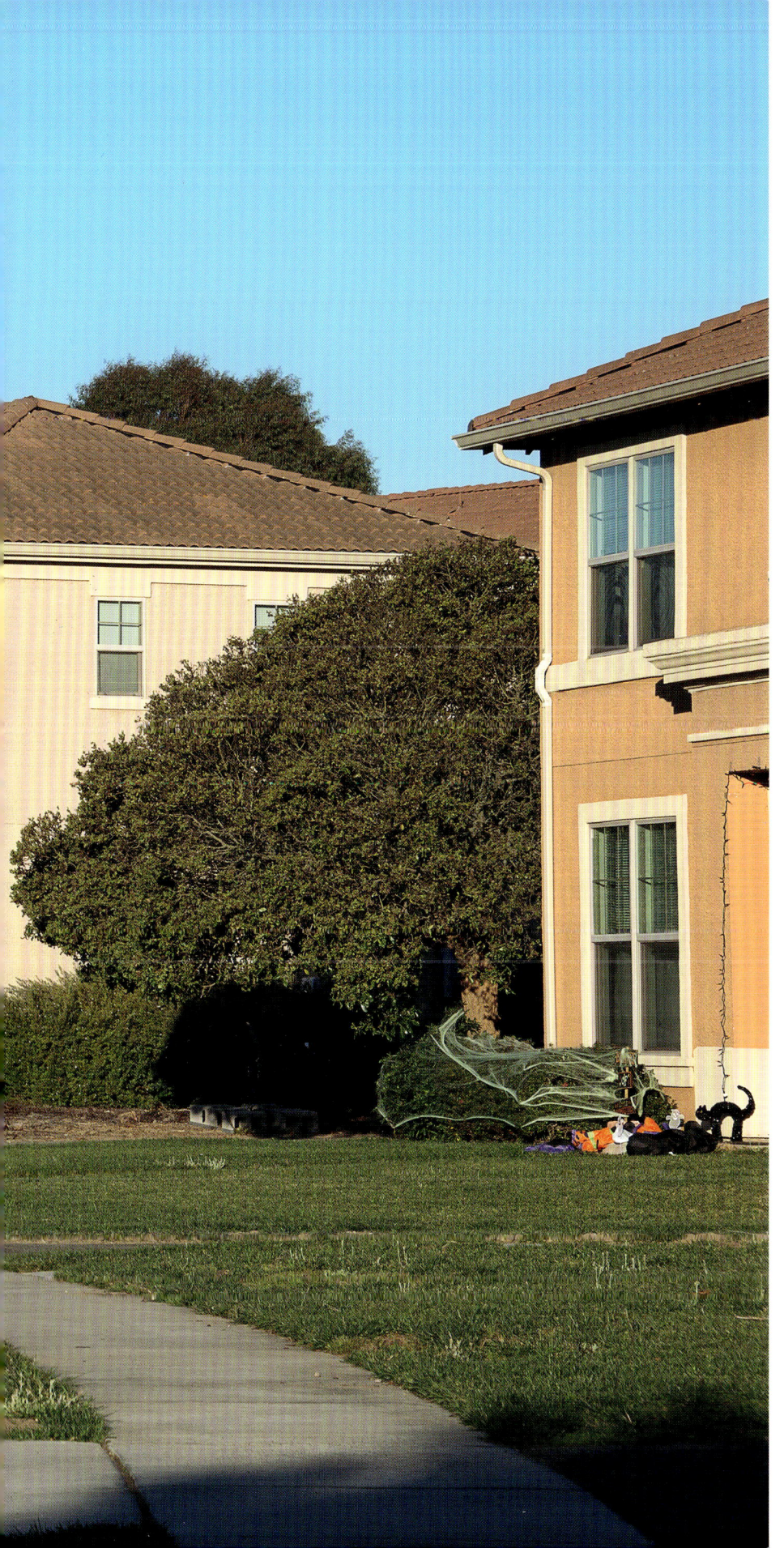

Halloween Decorations, Seaside, CA – 2017

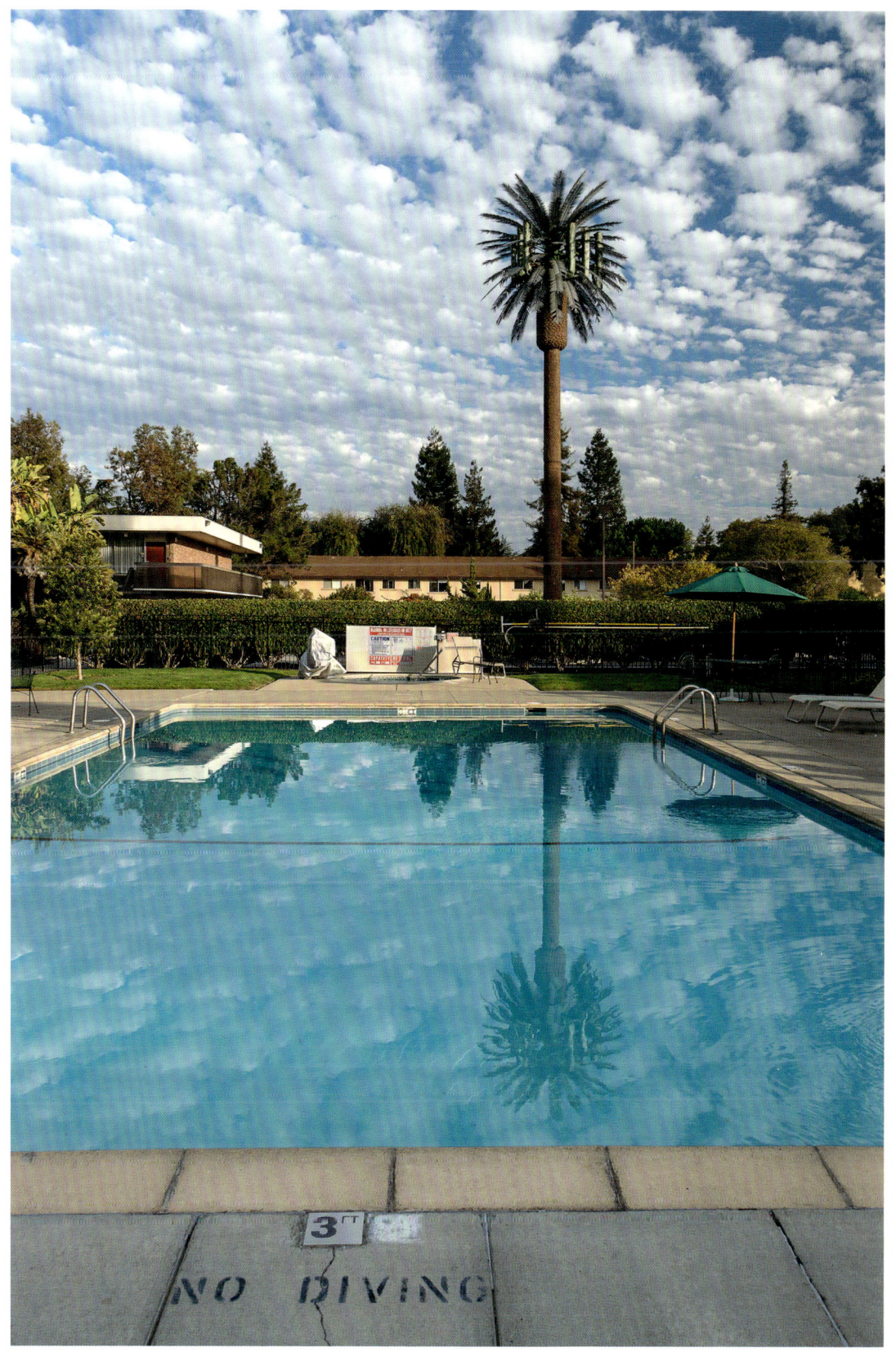

Hotel Pool, Sunnyvale, CA – 2016

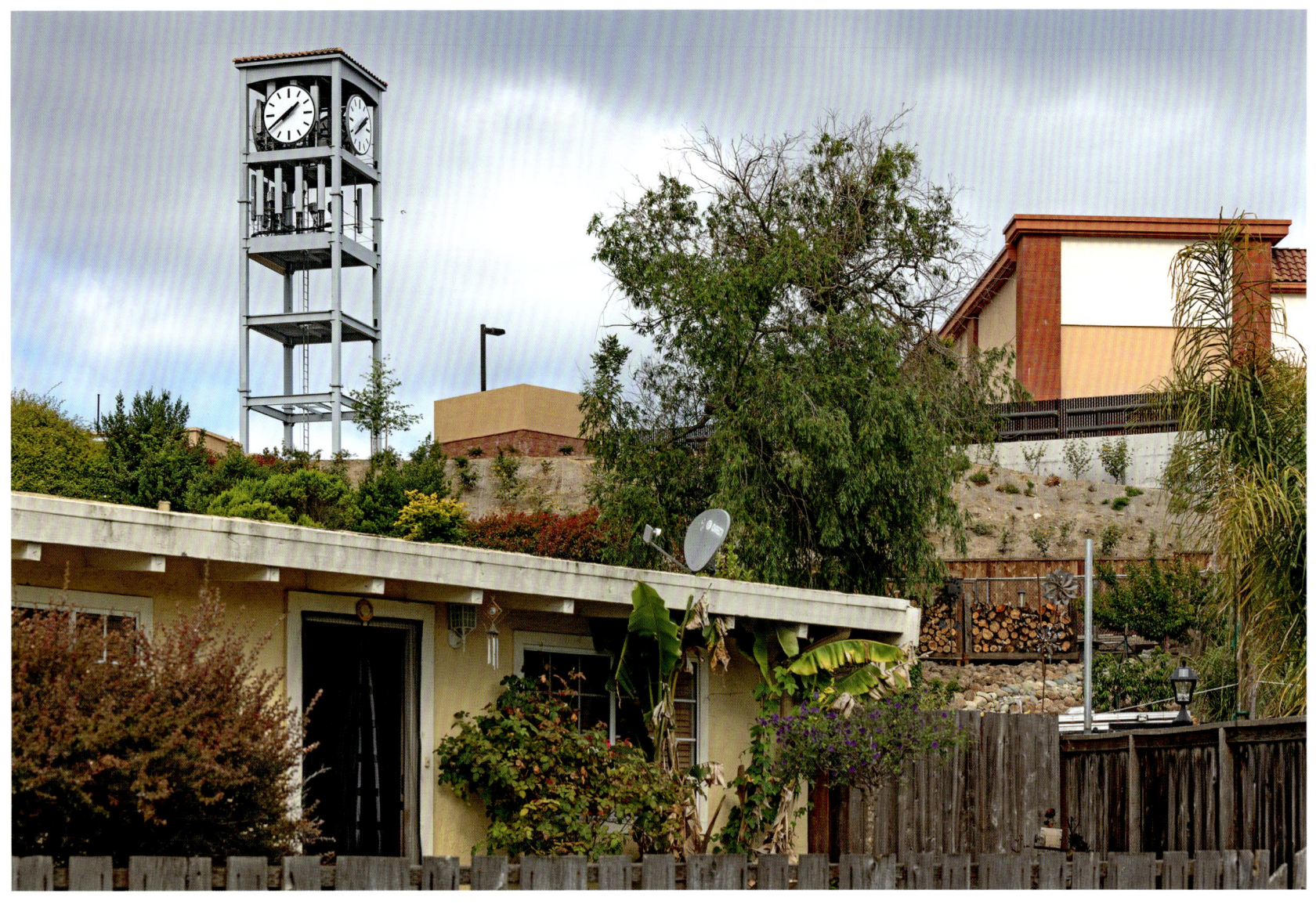

Clock Tower, Pinole, CA – 2020

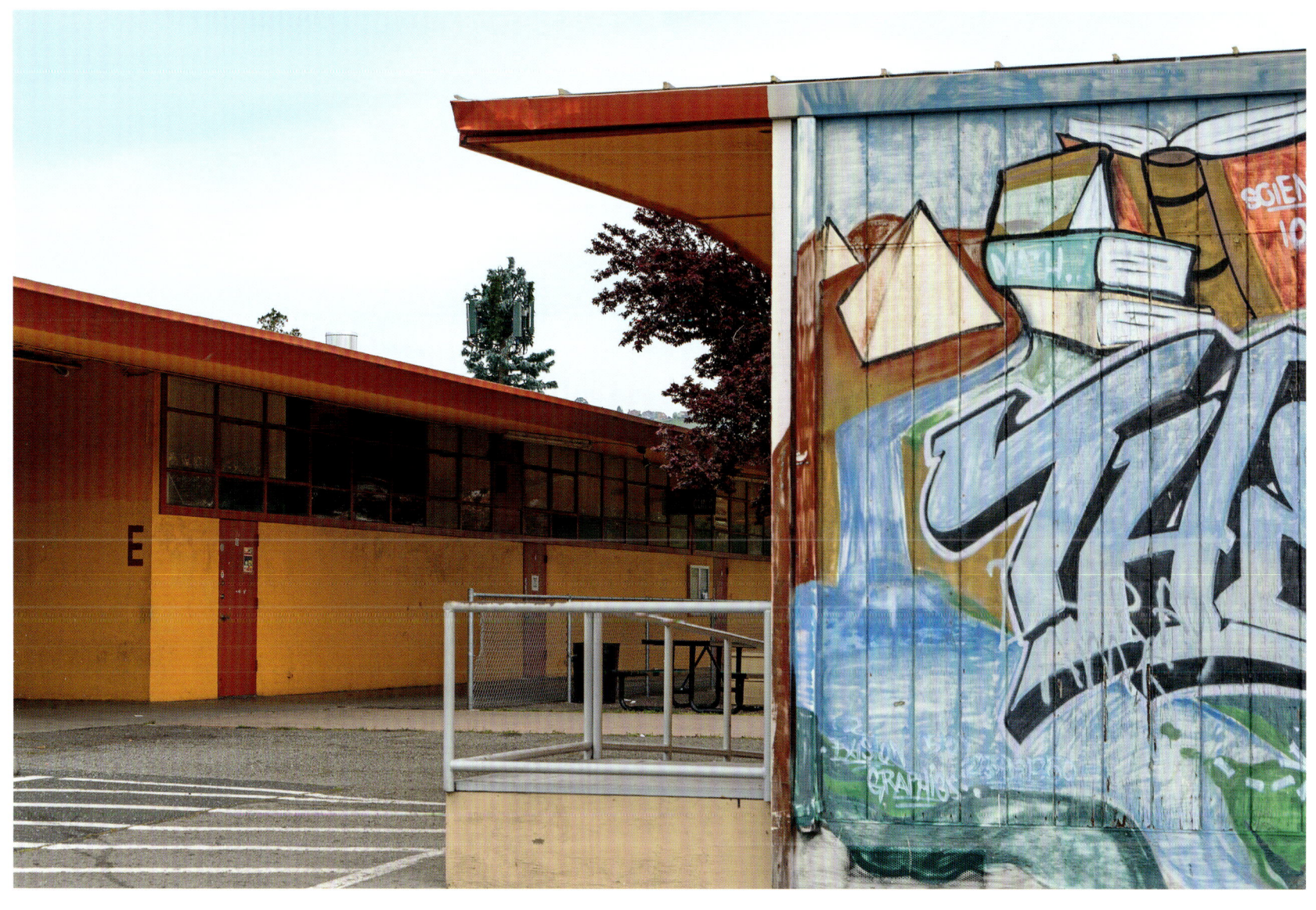

Elementary School, Hayward, CA – 2017

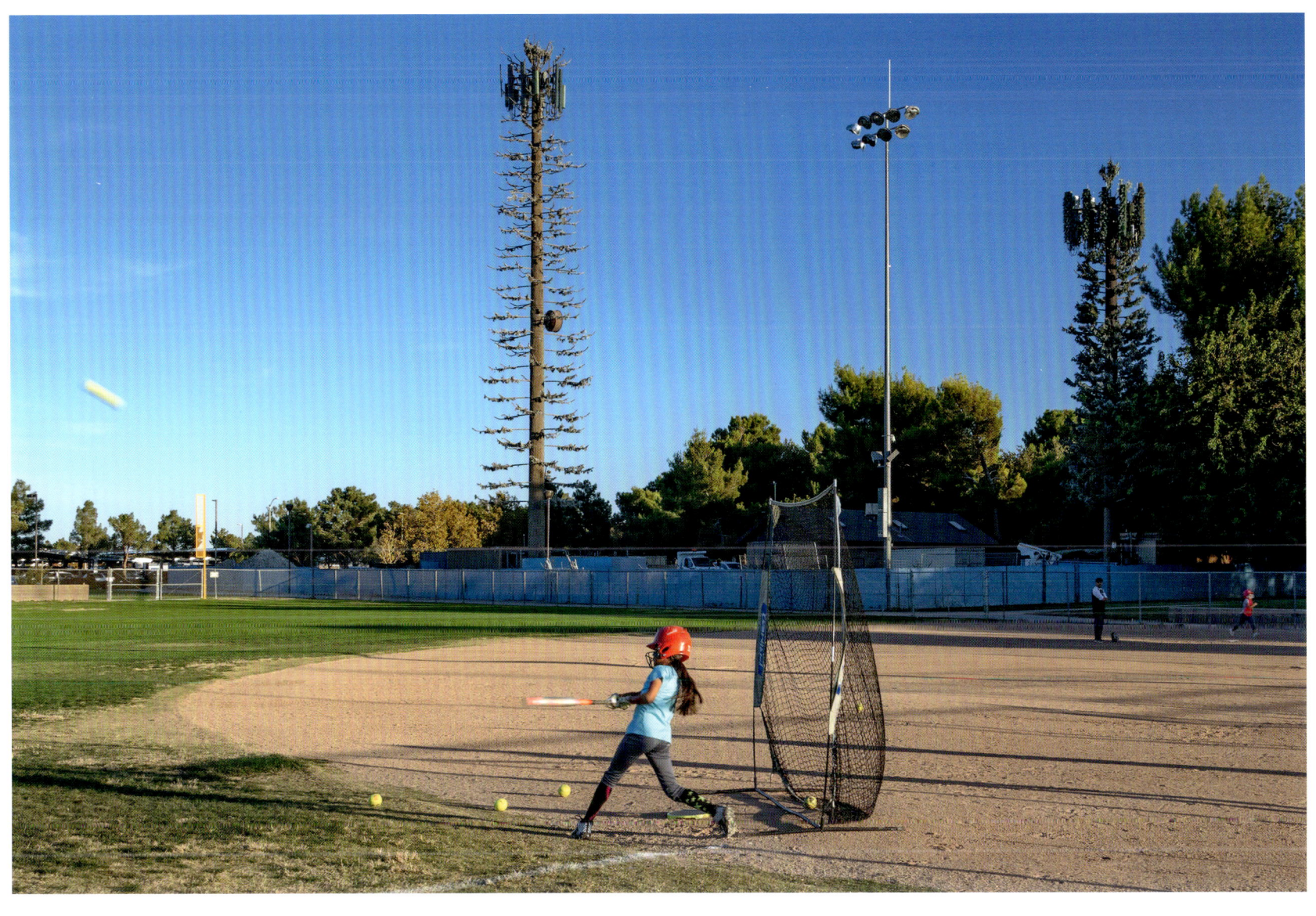

Softball Practice, Lancaster, CA – 2019

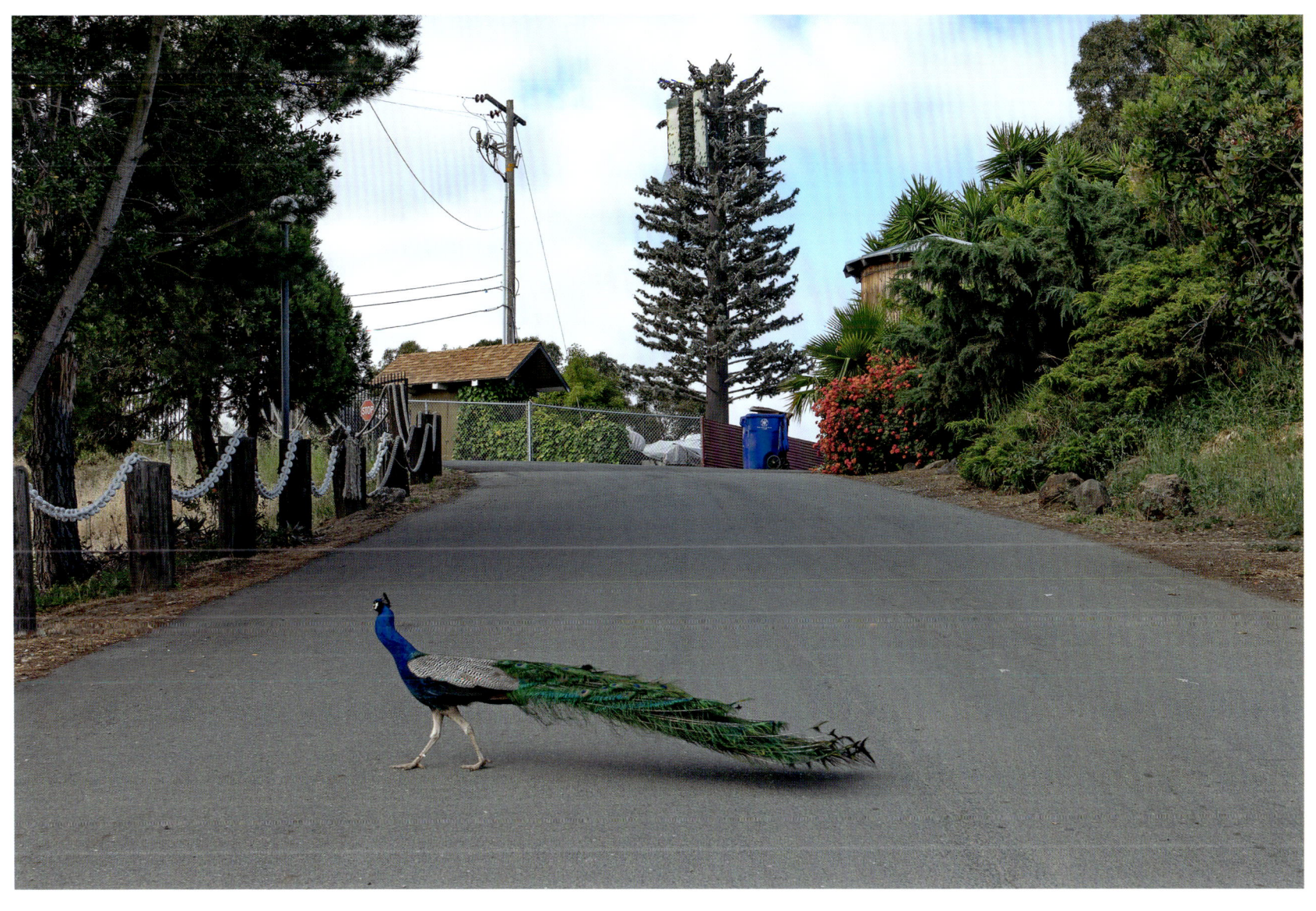

Superfluous Plumage, Rodeo, CA – 2020

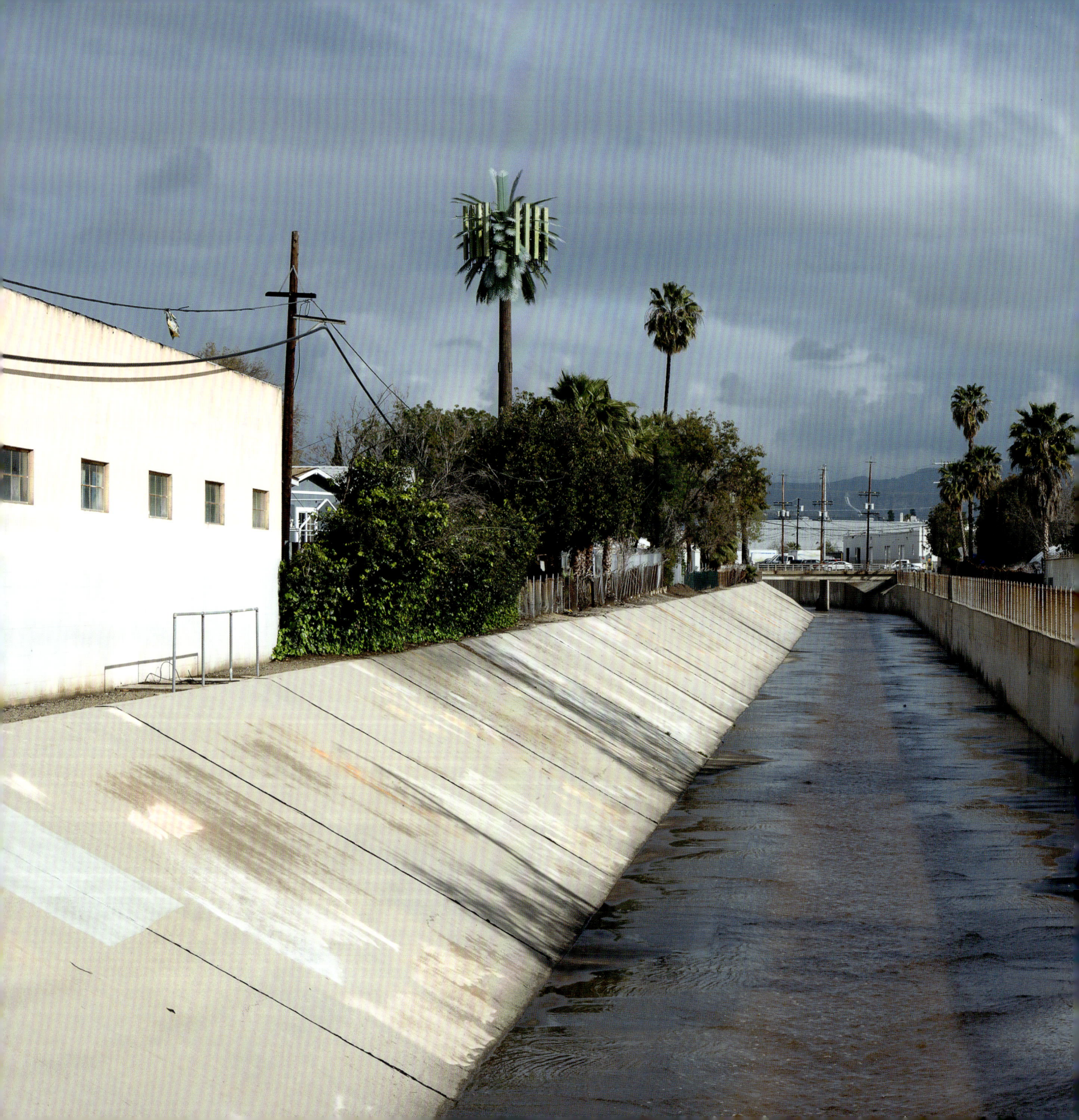

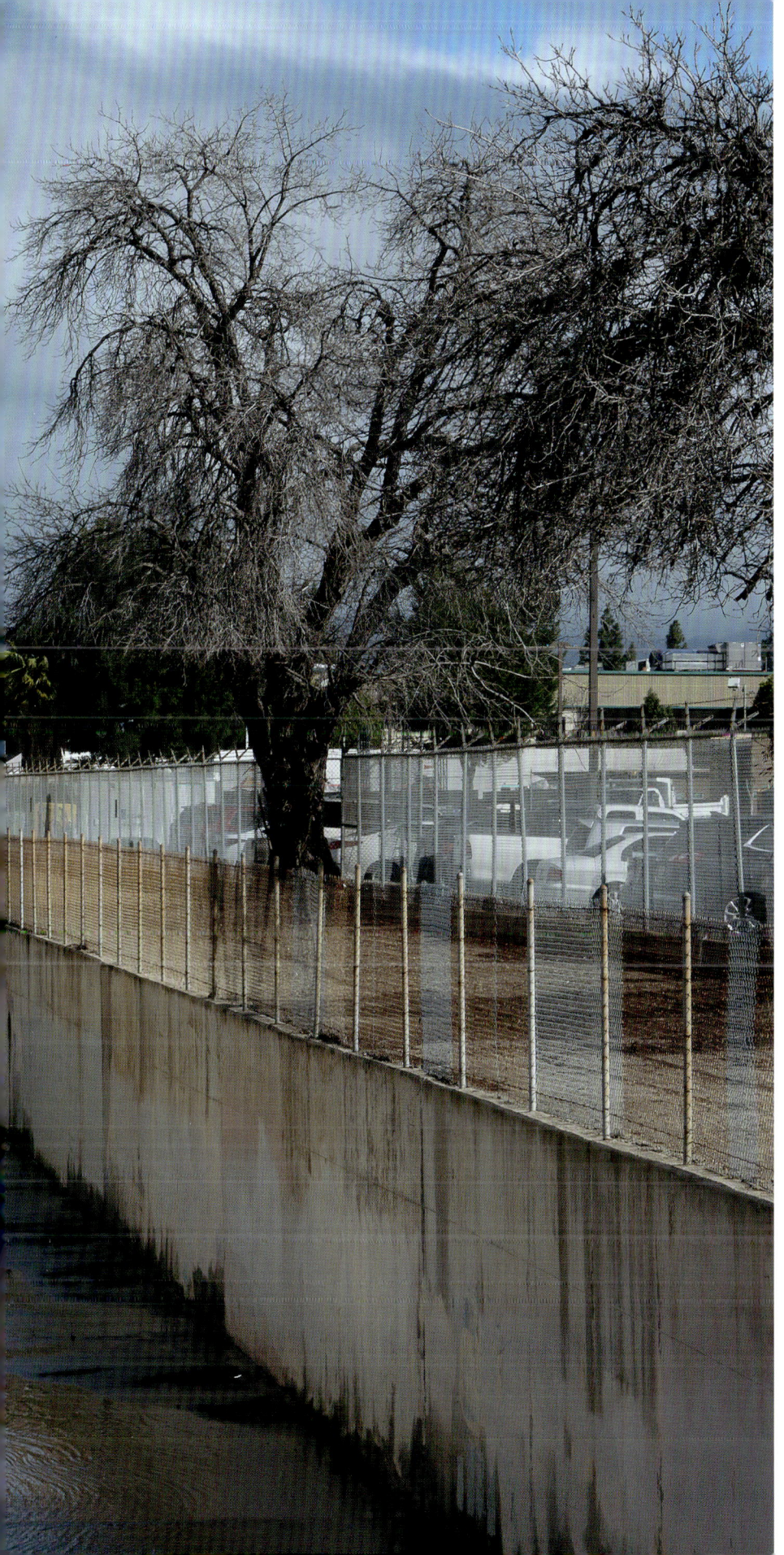

Sometimes It Rains in Southern California, Van Nuys, CA – 2019

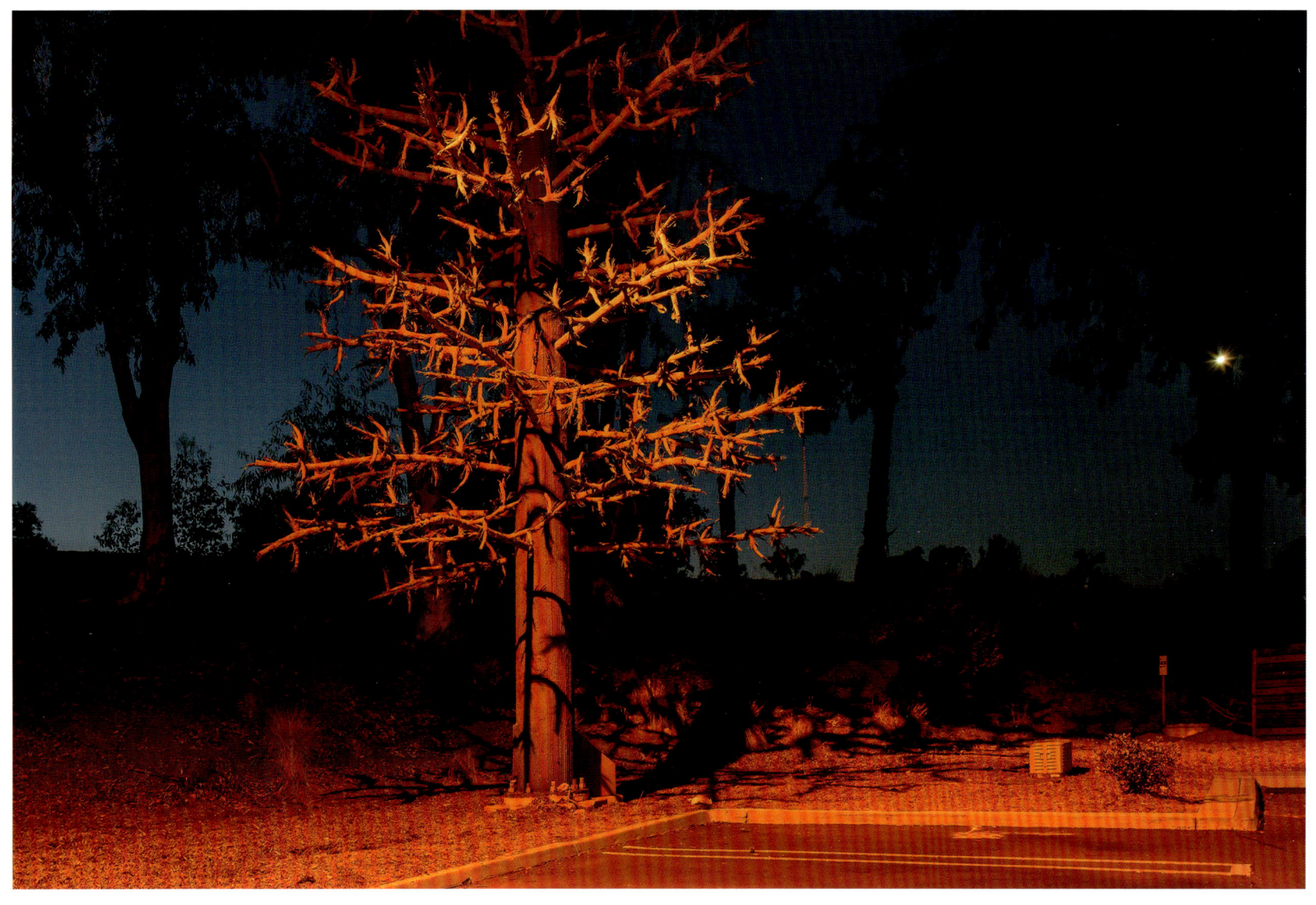

Geriatric Evergreen in the Preschool Parking Lot, La Mesa, CA – 2018

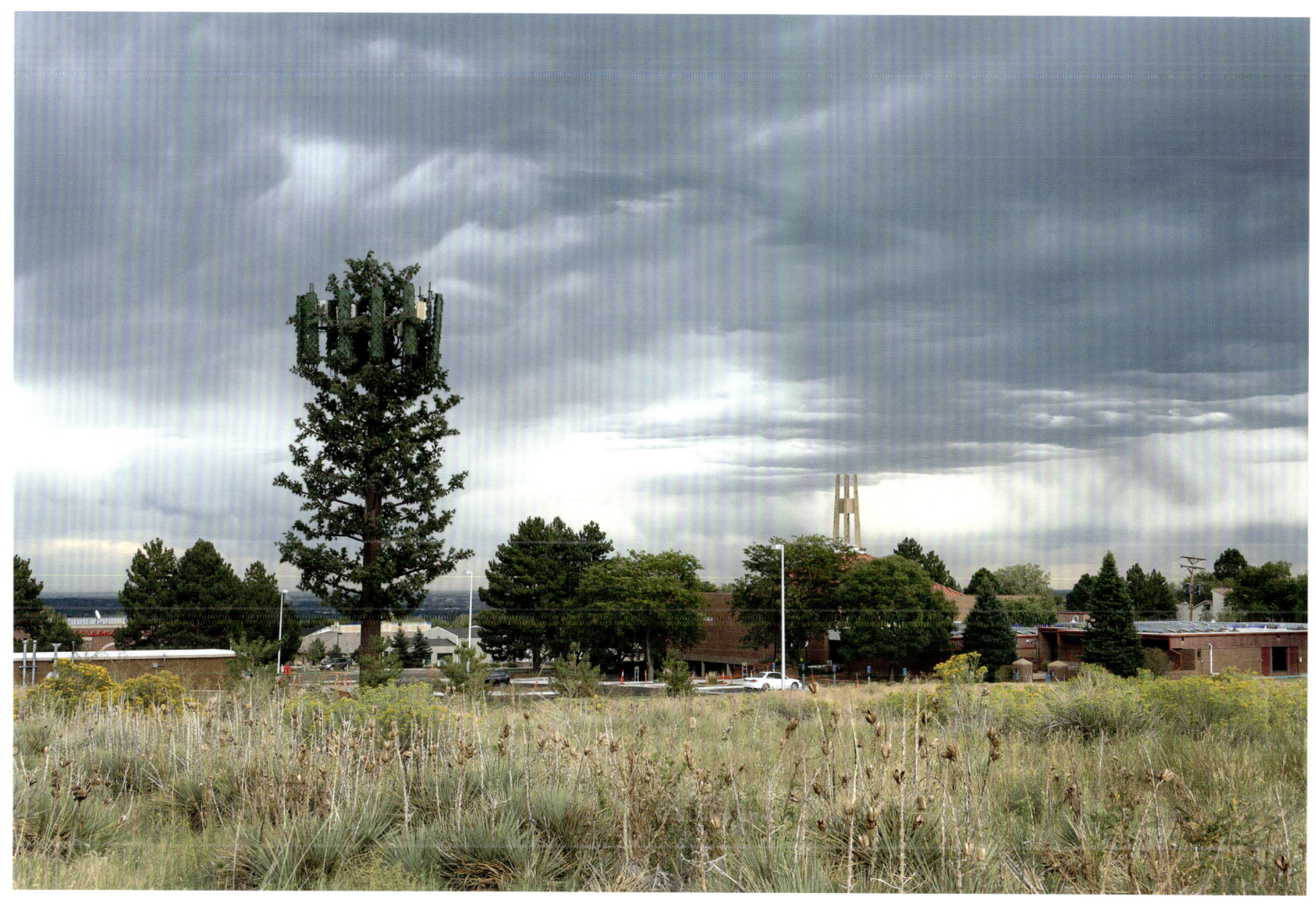

Incoming Storm, Lakewood, CO – 2018

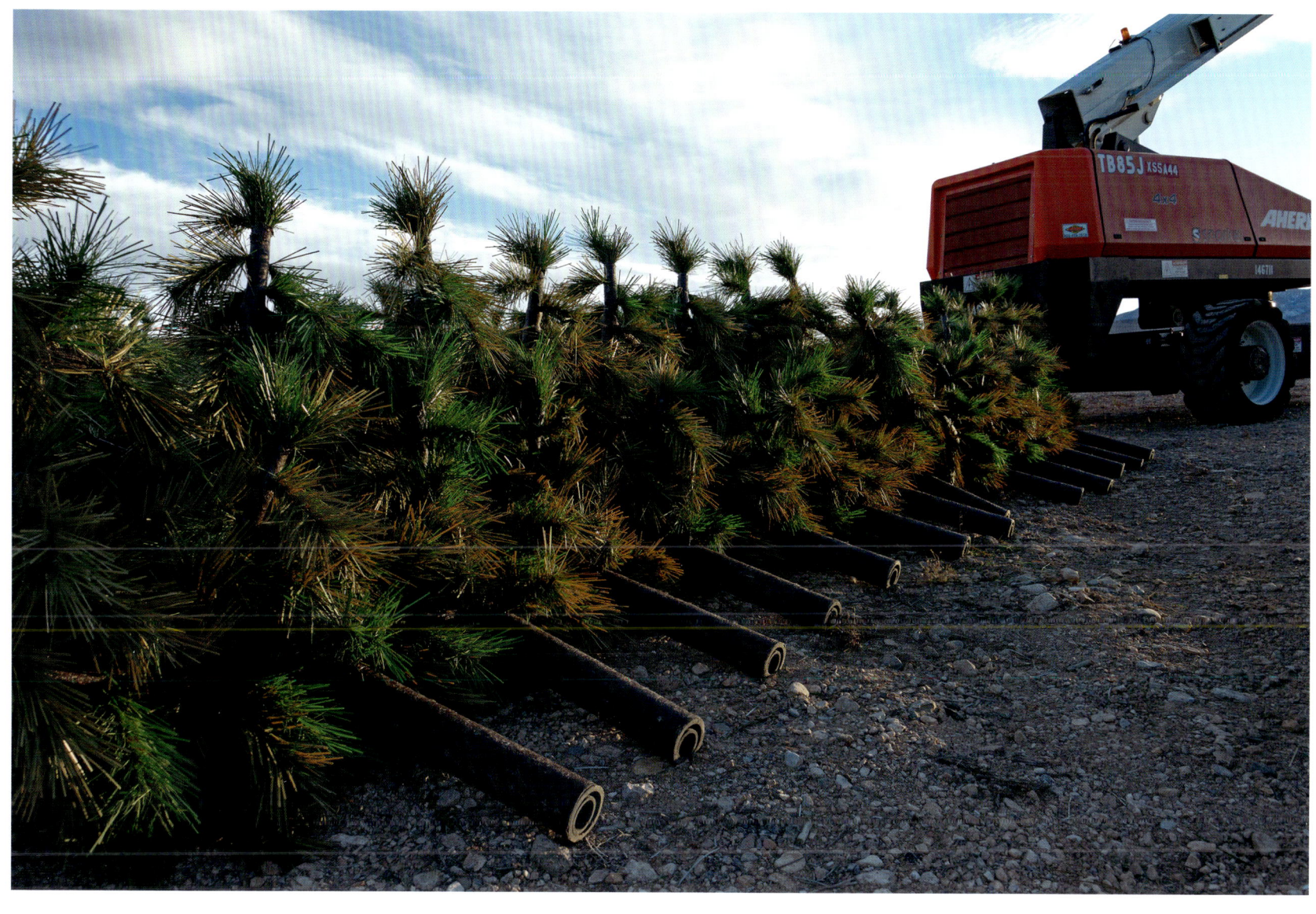

Refurb, Blue Diamond, NV – 2019

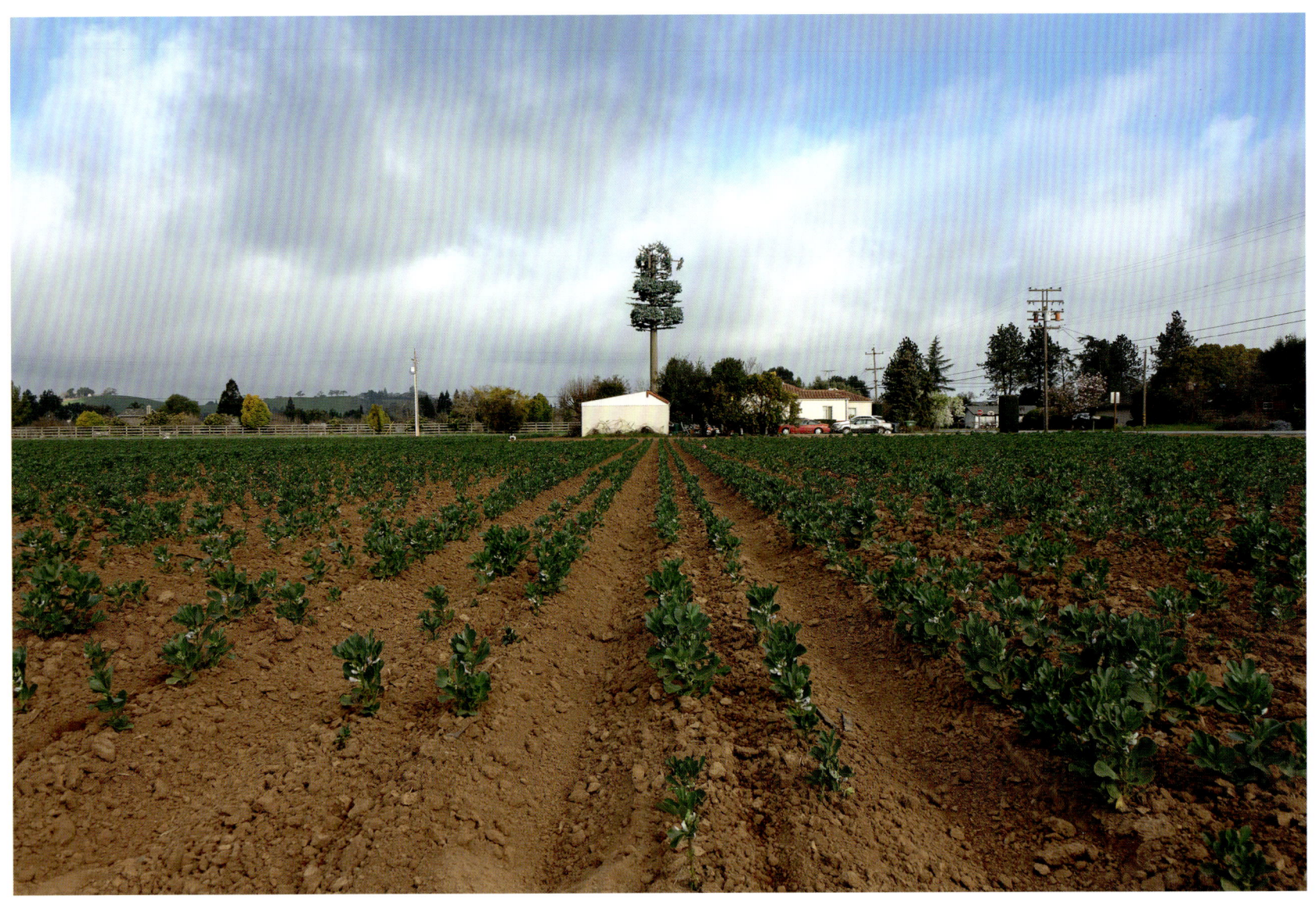

Harvest, San Martin, CA – 2020

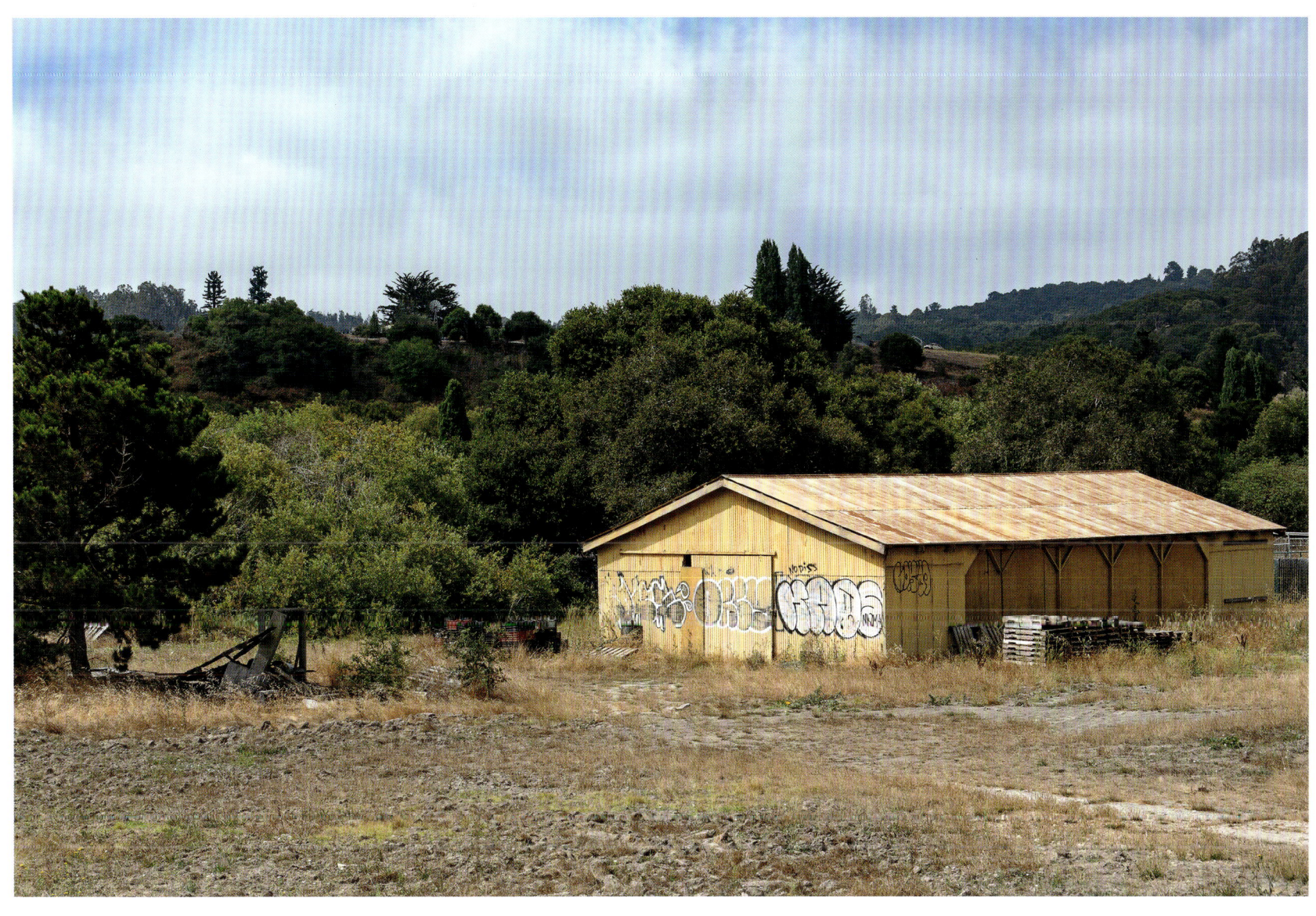

Graffiti, Aromas, CA – 2020

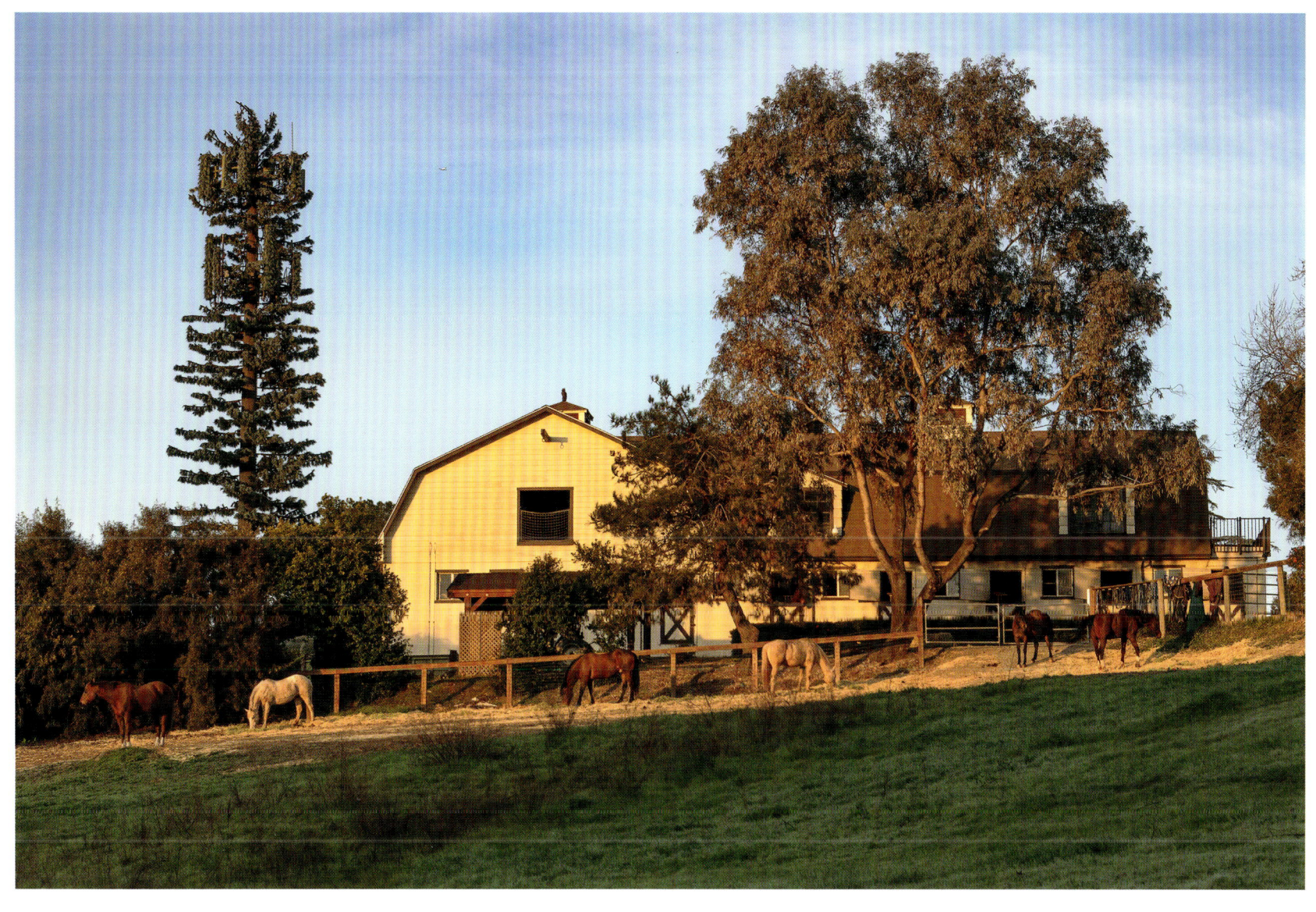

Equine Sunrise, Los Altos Hills, CA – 2020

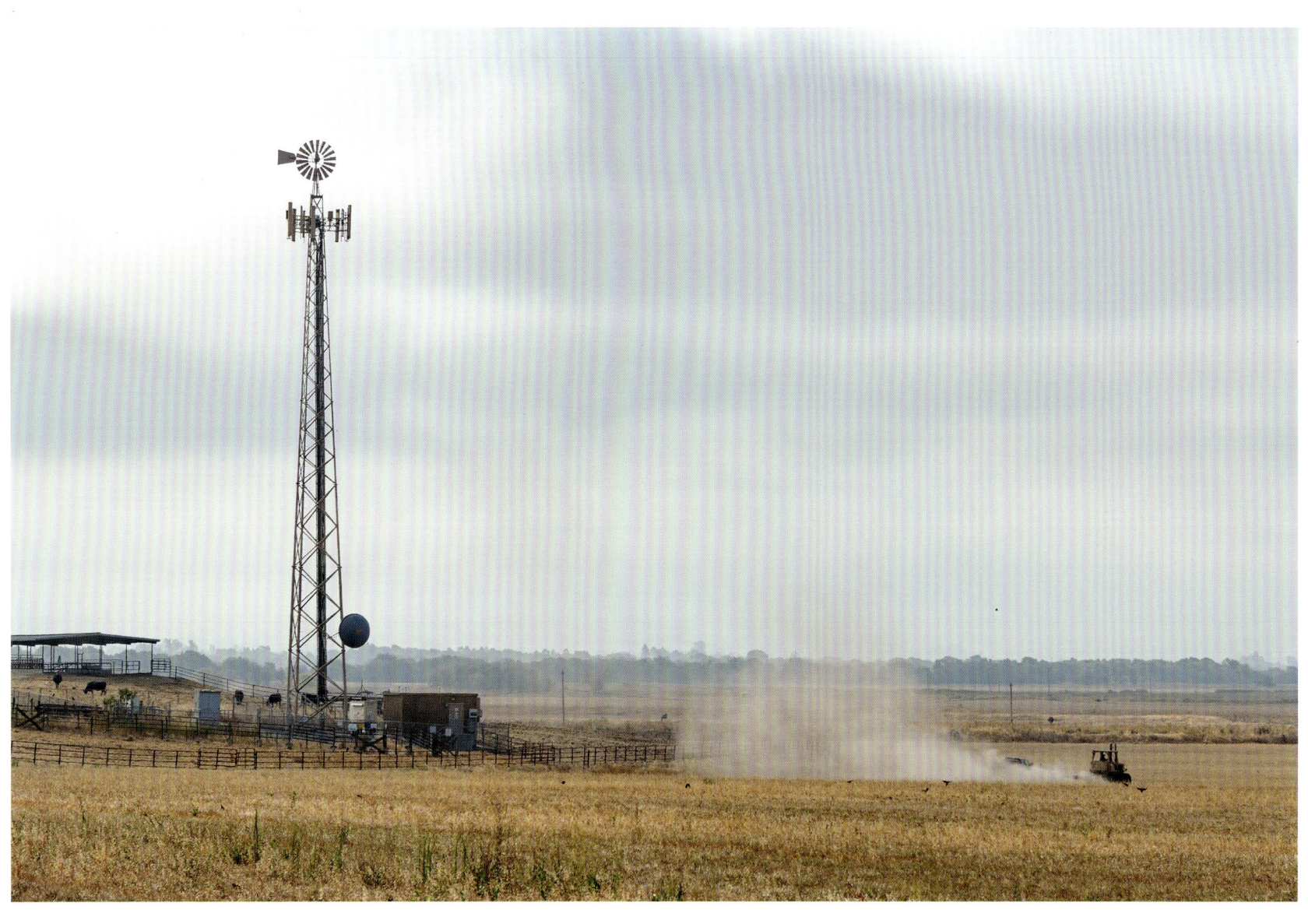

Windmill, Gilroy, CA – 2020

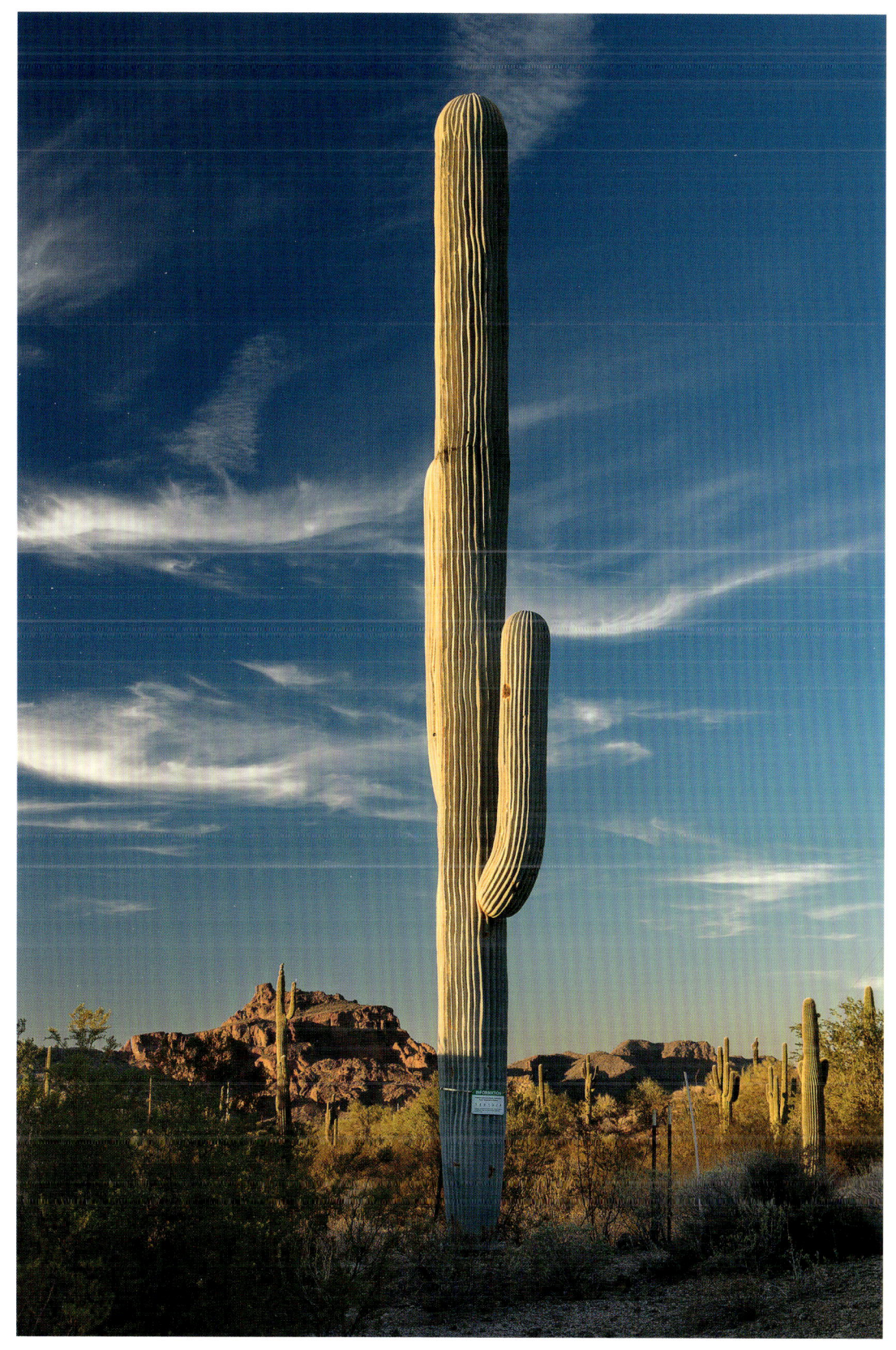

Golden Hour Saguaro, Mesa, AZ – 2016

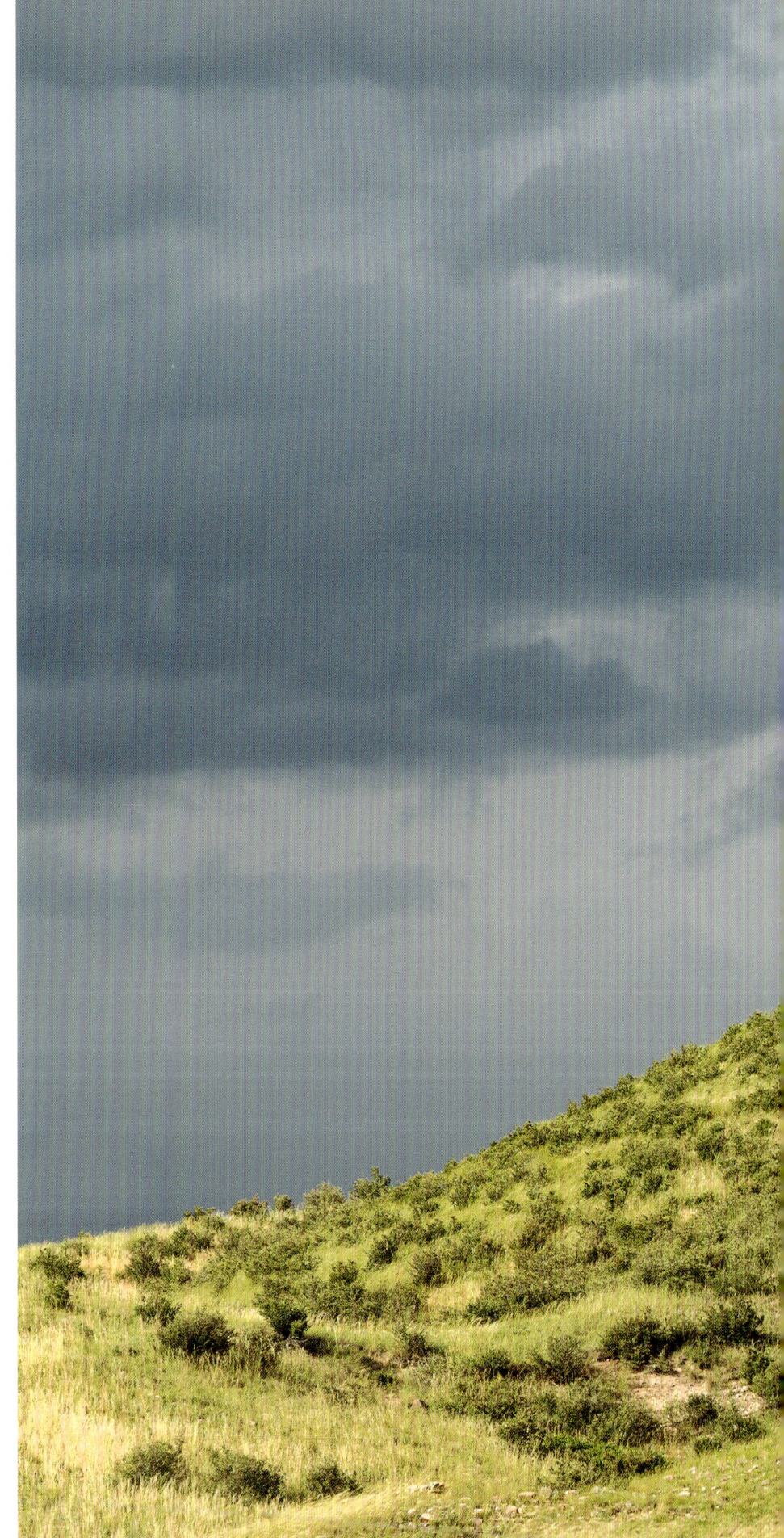

Bison Sign, WY/CO Border – 2018

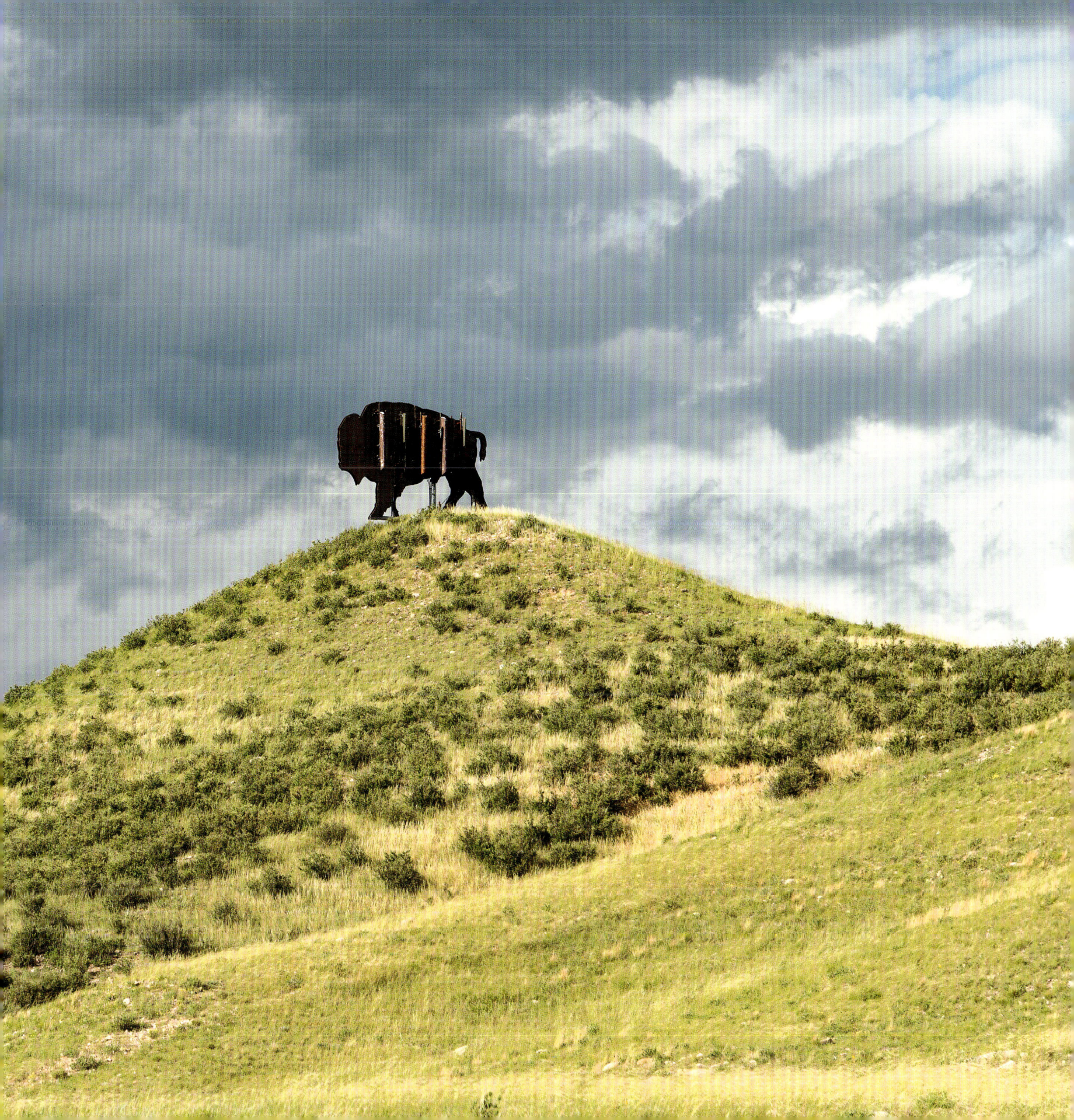

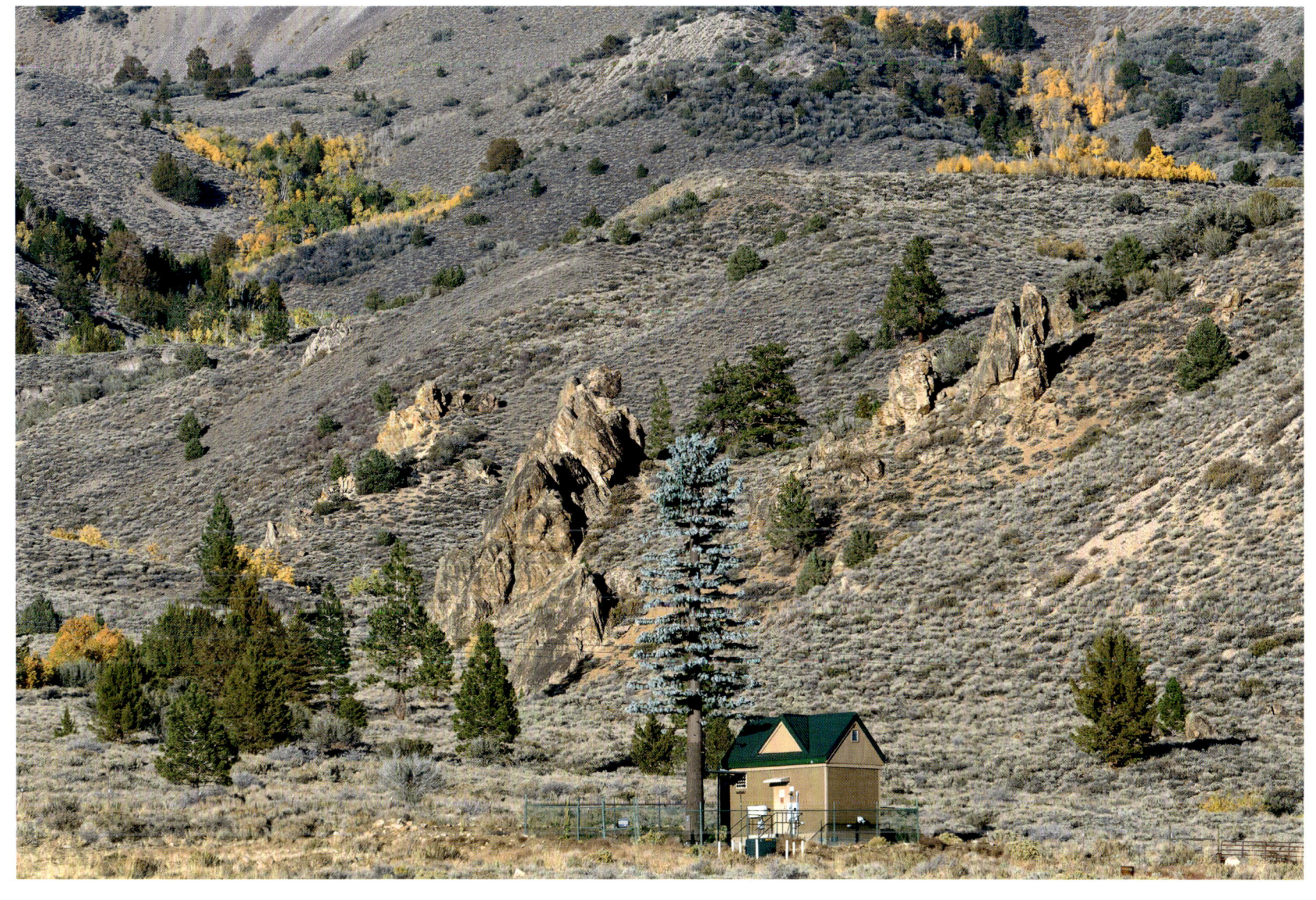

Early Autumn Color, Sonora Junction, CA – 2014

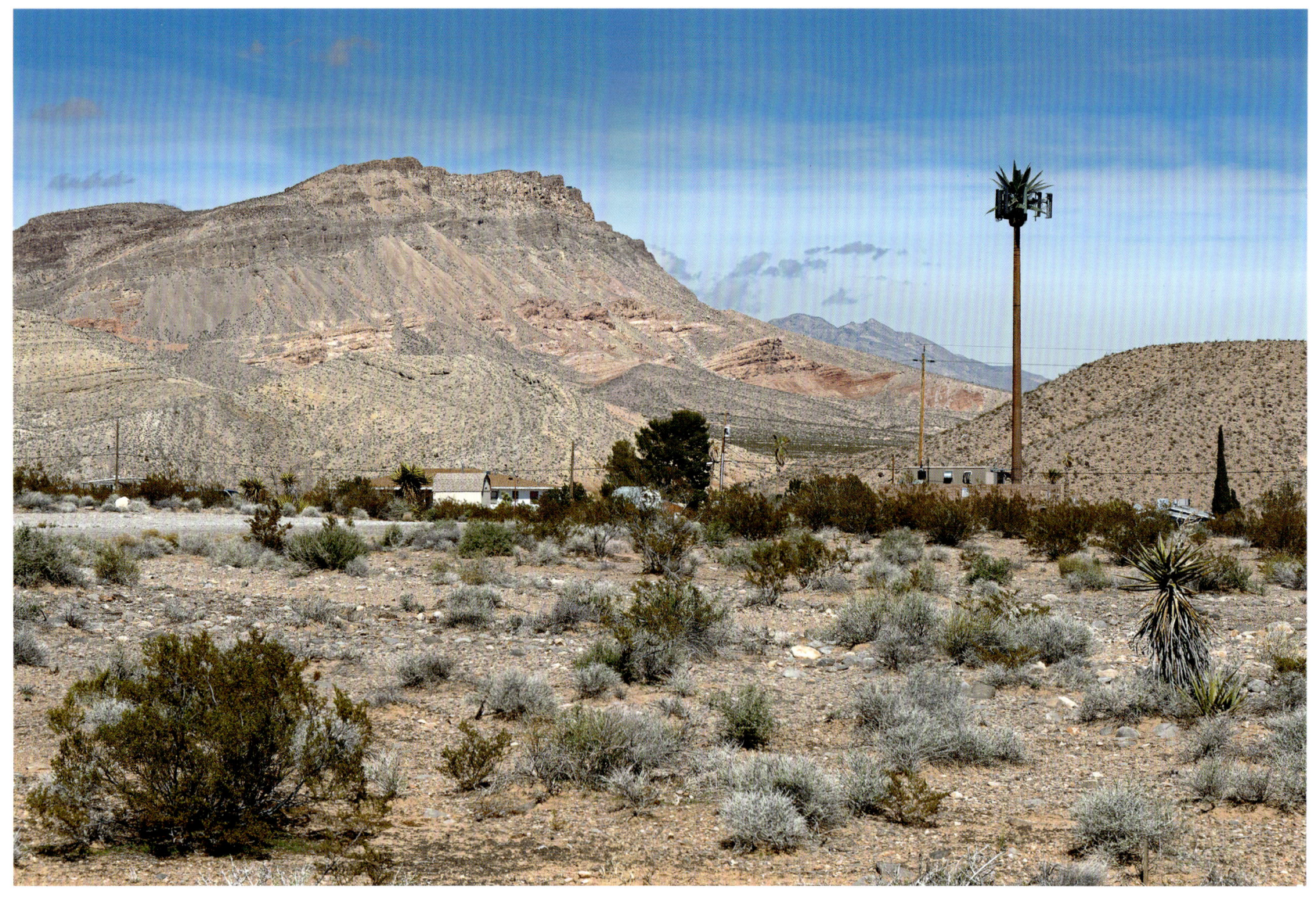

Desert Palm, Blue Diamond, NV – 2019

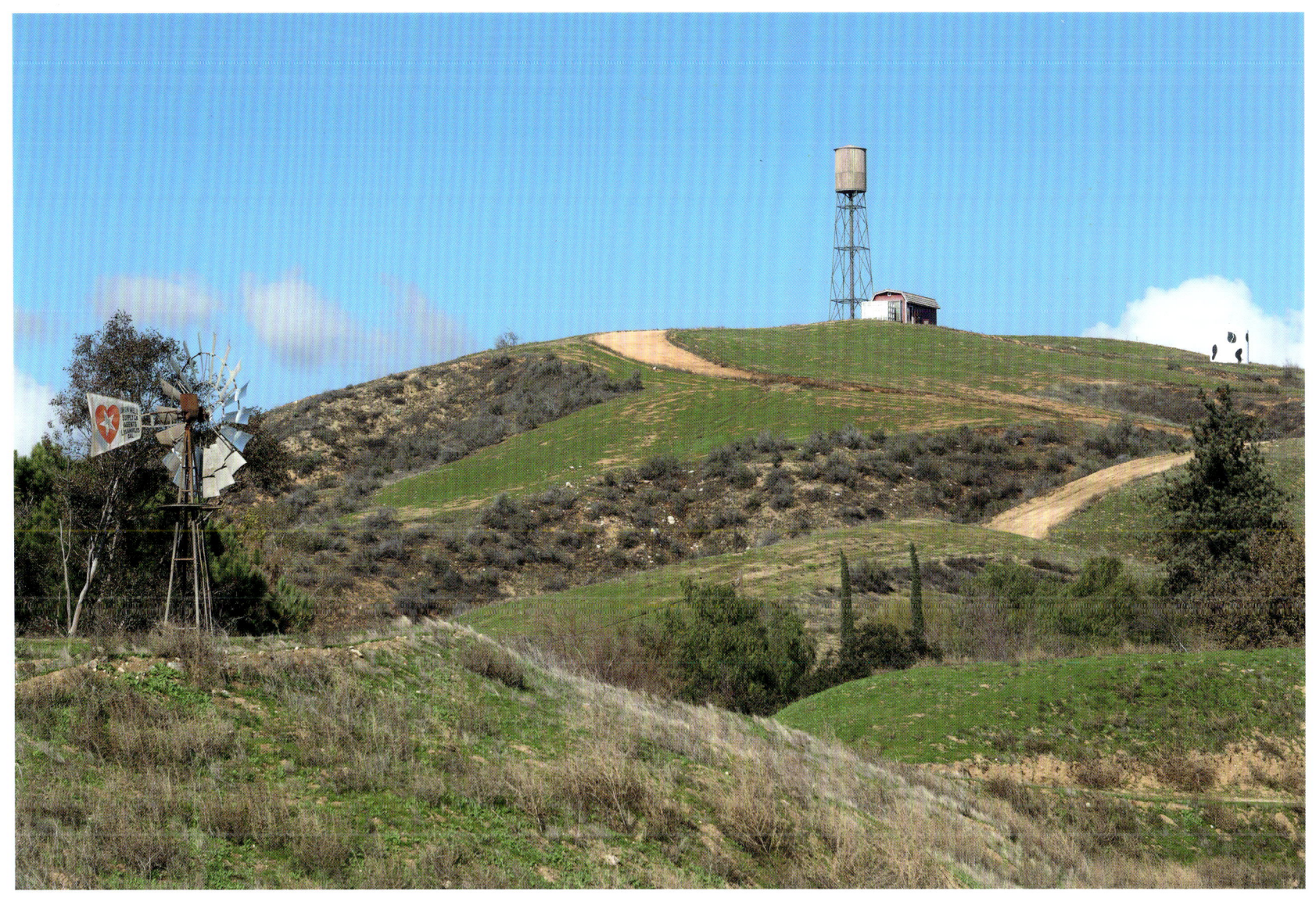

Top of the Hill Water Tower, Calimesa, CA – 2017

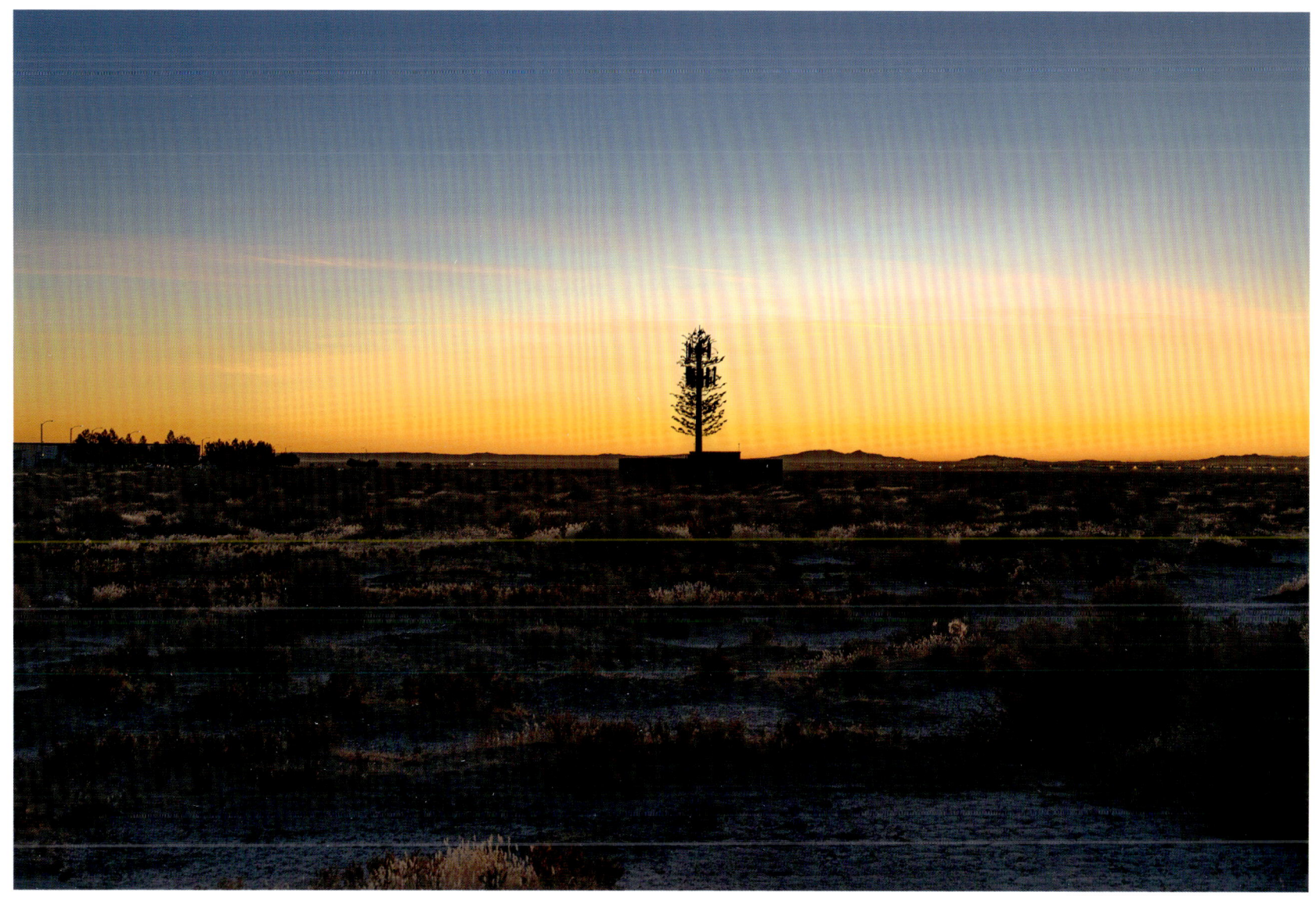

High Desert Sunrise, Lancaster, CA – 2019

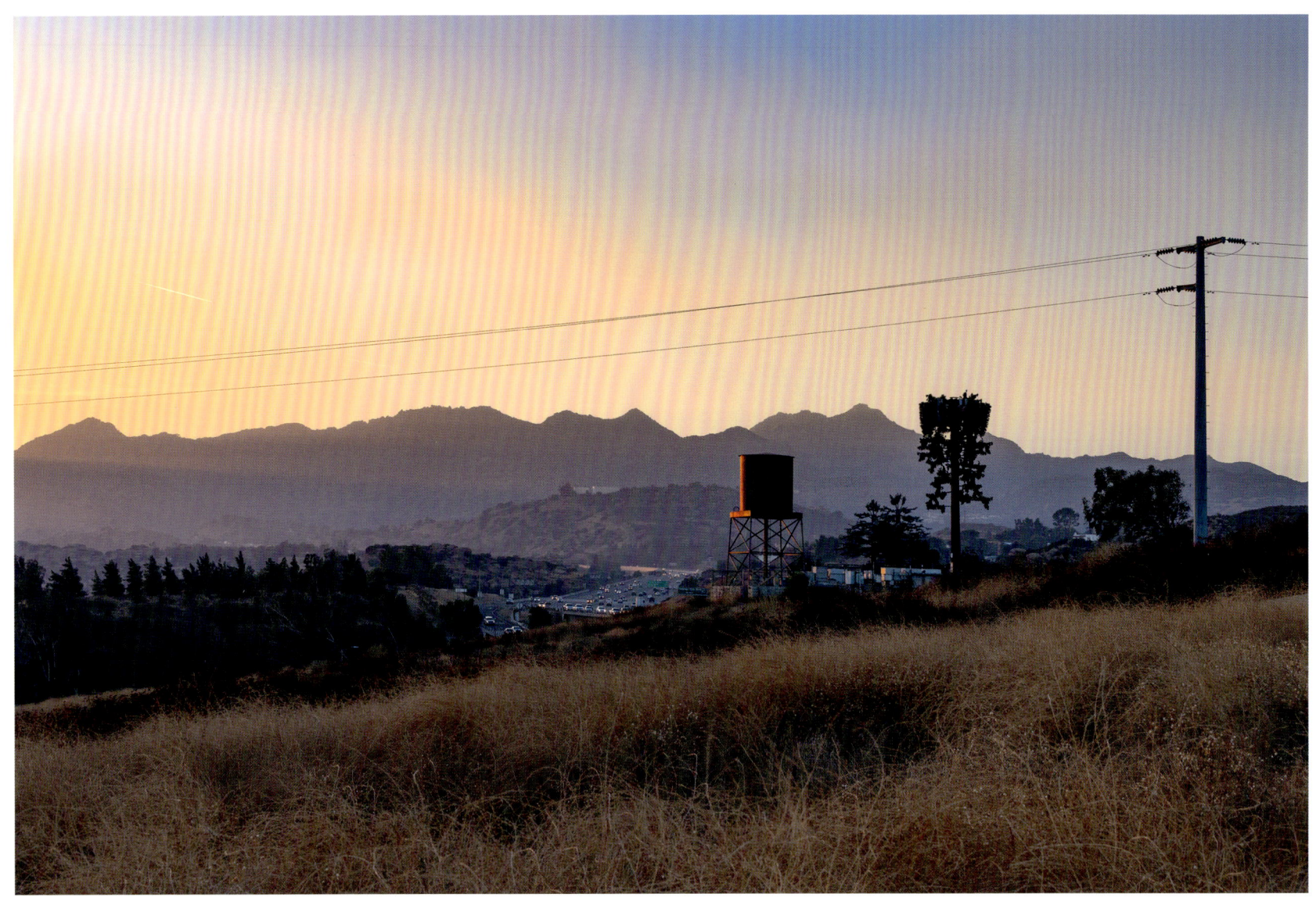

Smokey Sunset, Chatsworth, CA – 2019

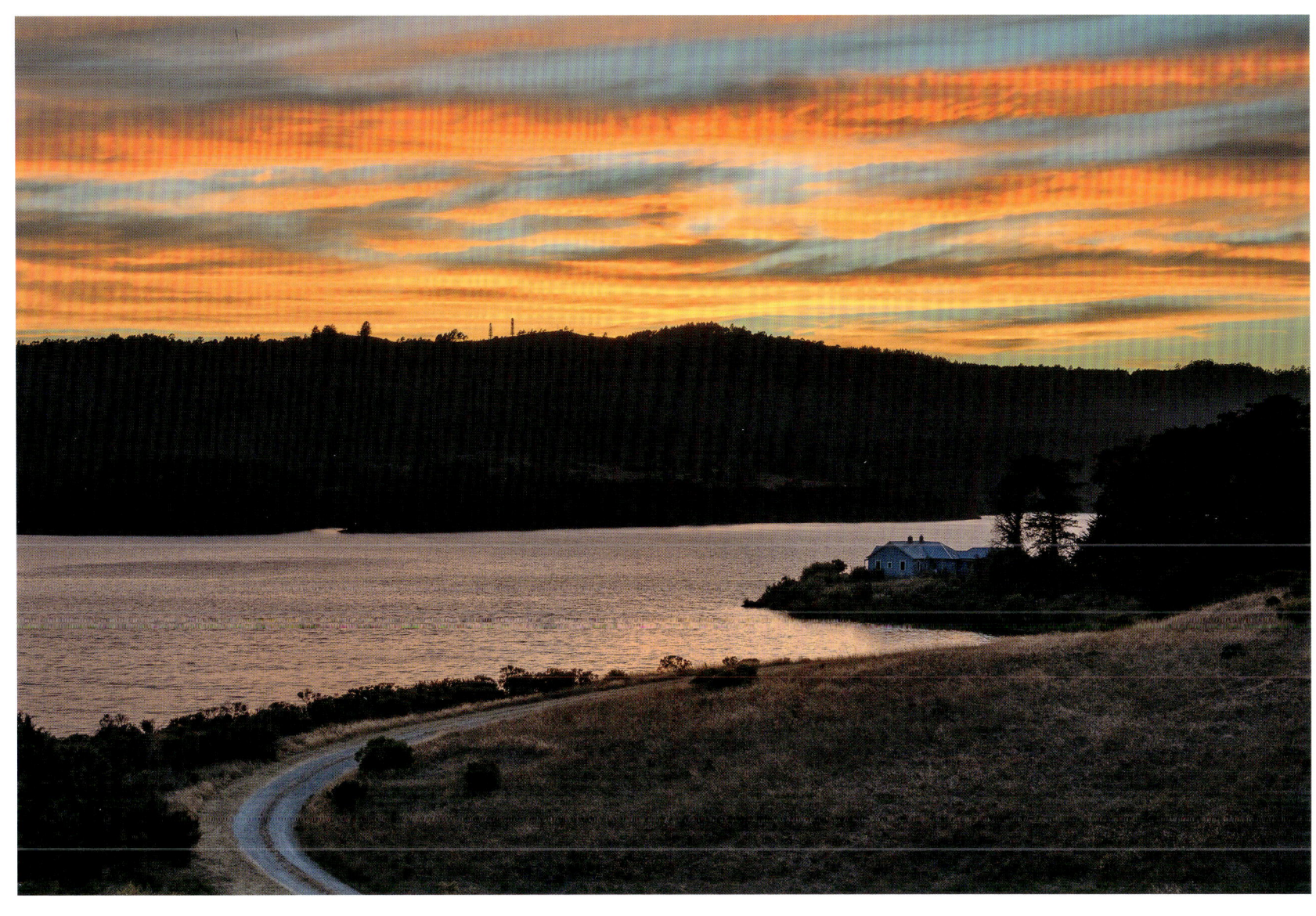

Above the San Andreas Fault, San Mateo County, CA – 2020

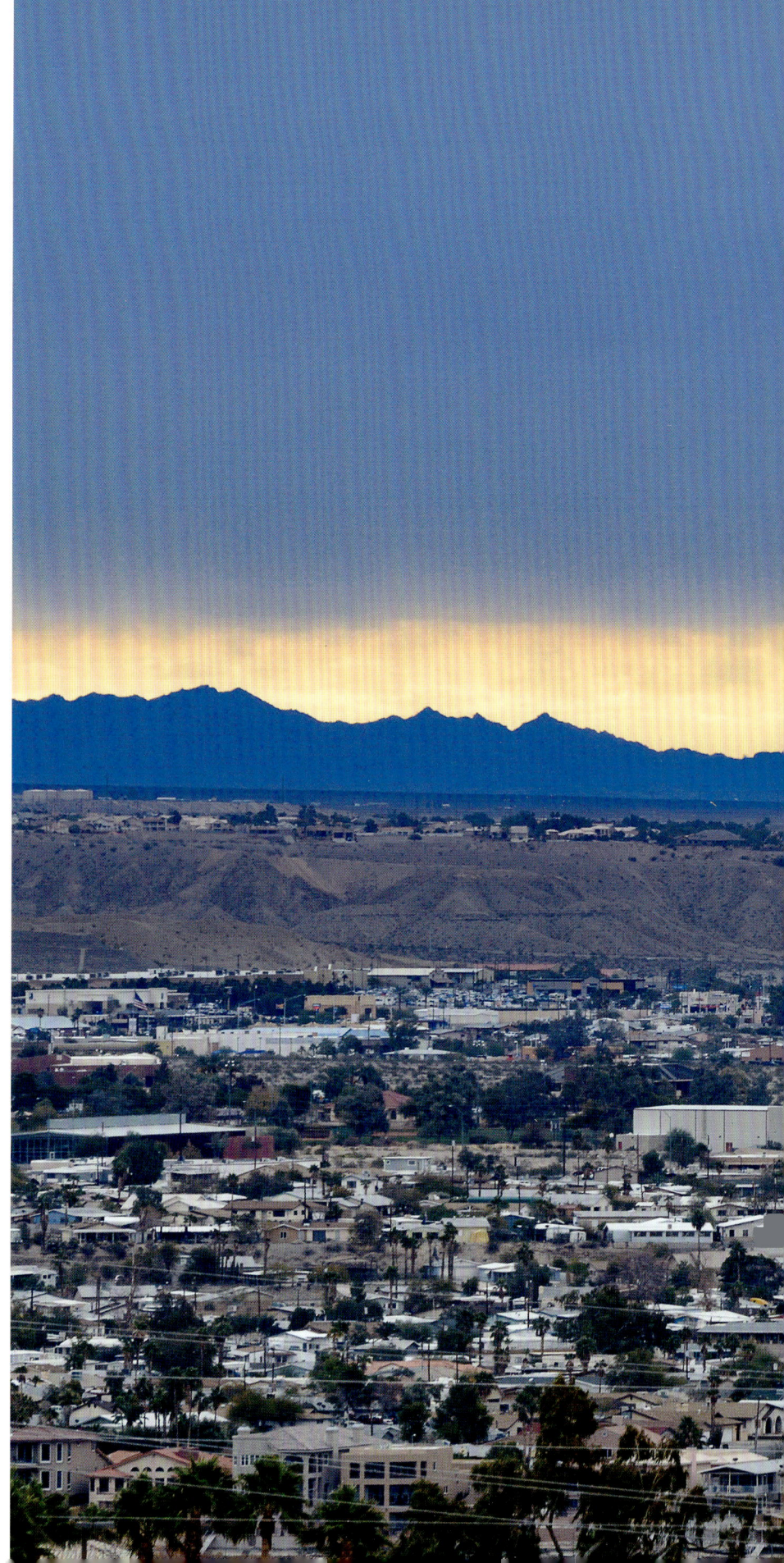

Passing Storm, Laughlin, NV – 2018

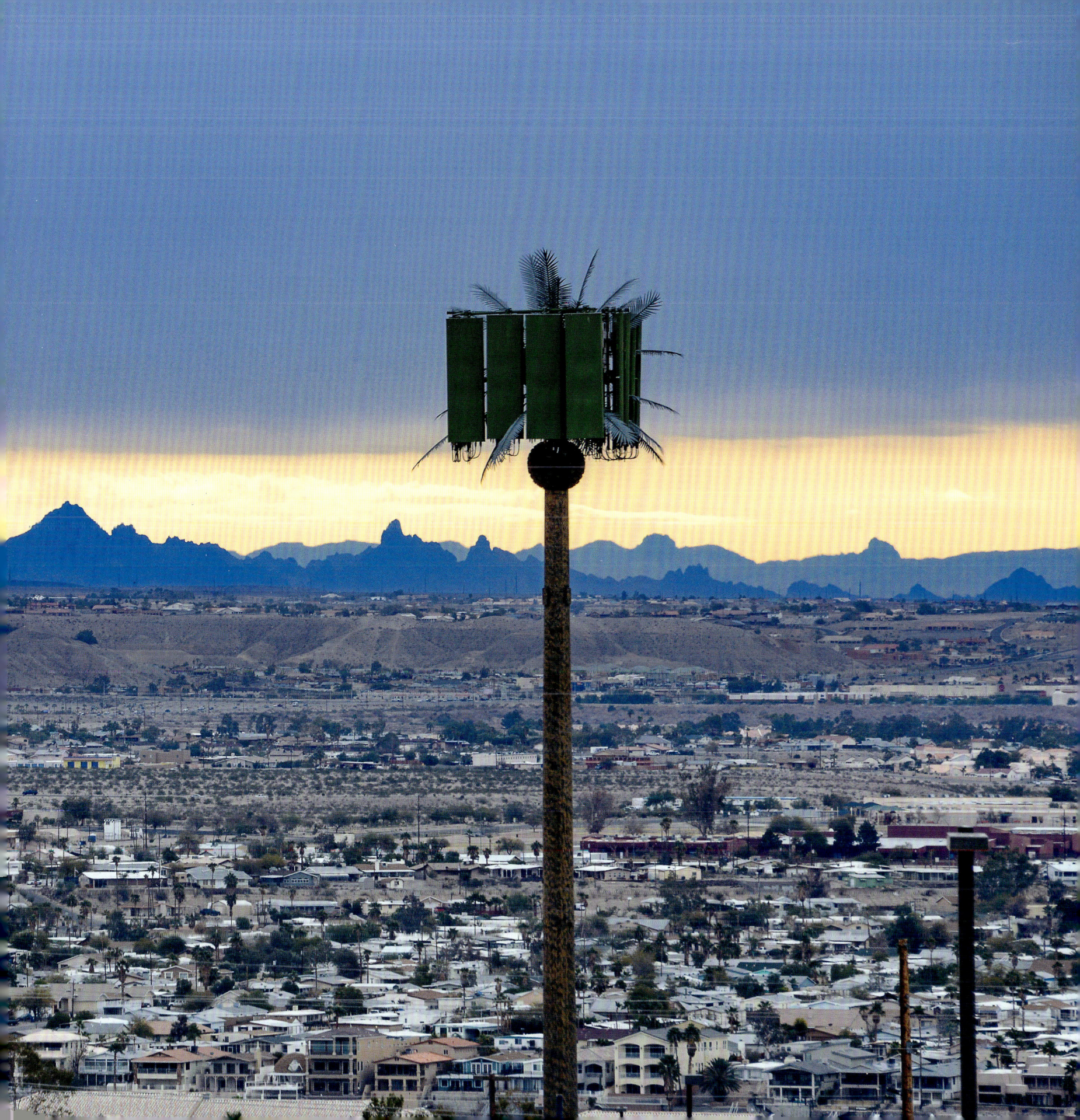

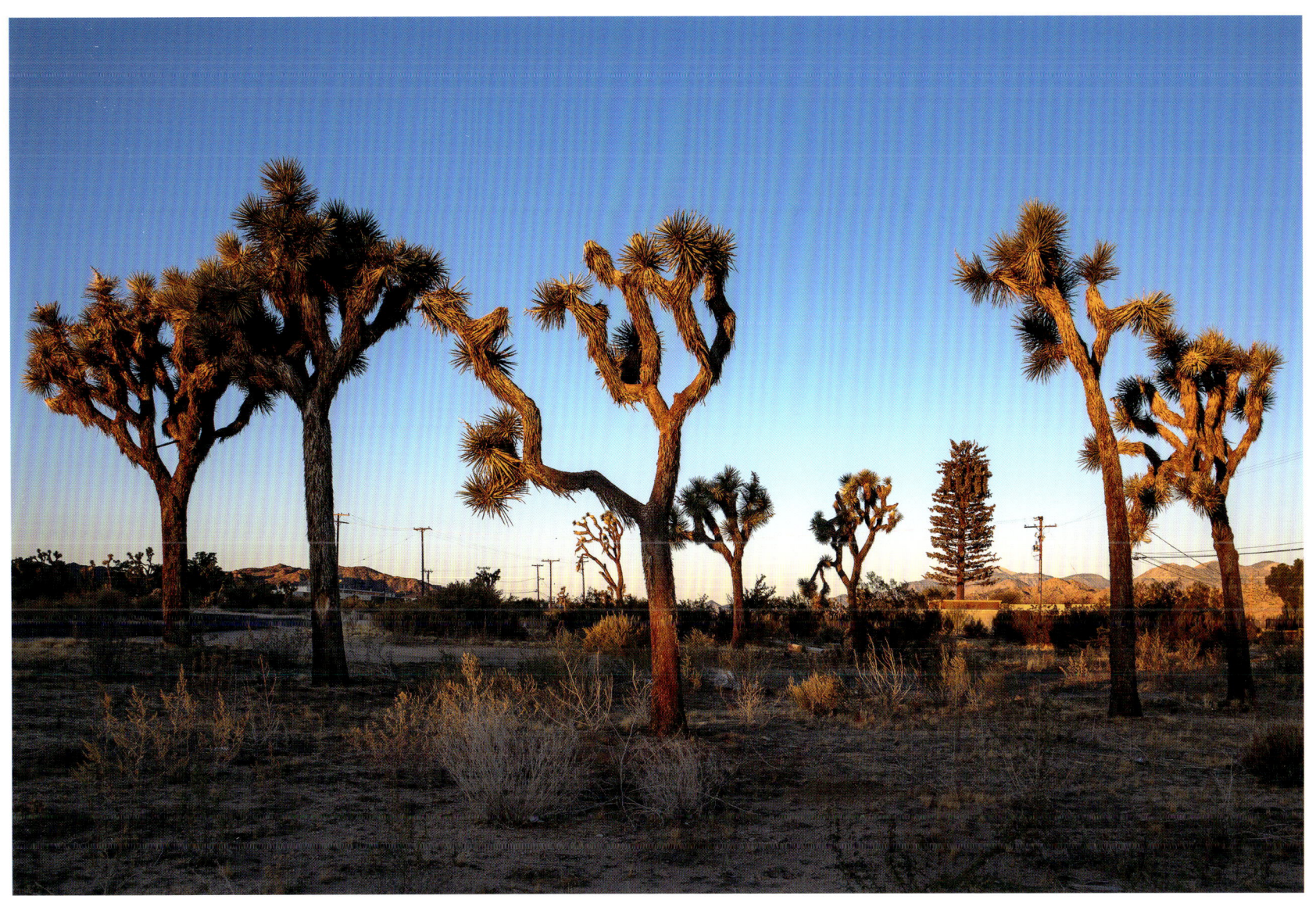

Not a Joshua Tree, Yucca Valley, CA – 2019

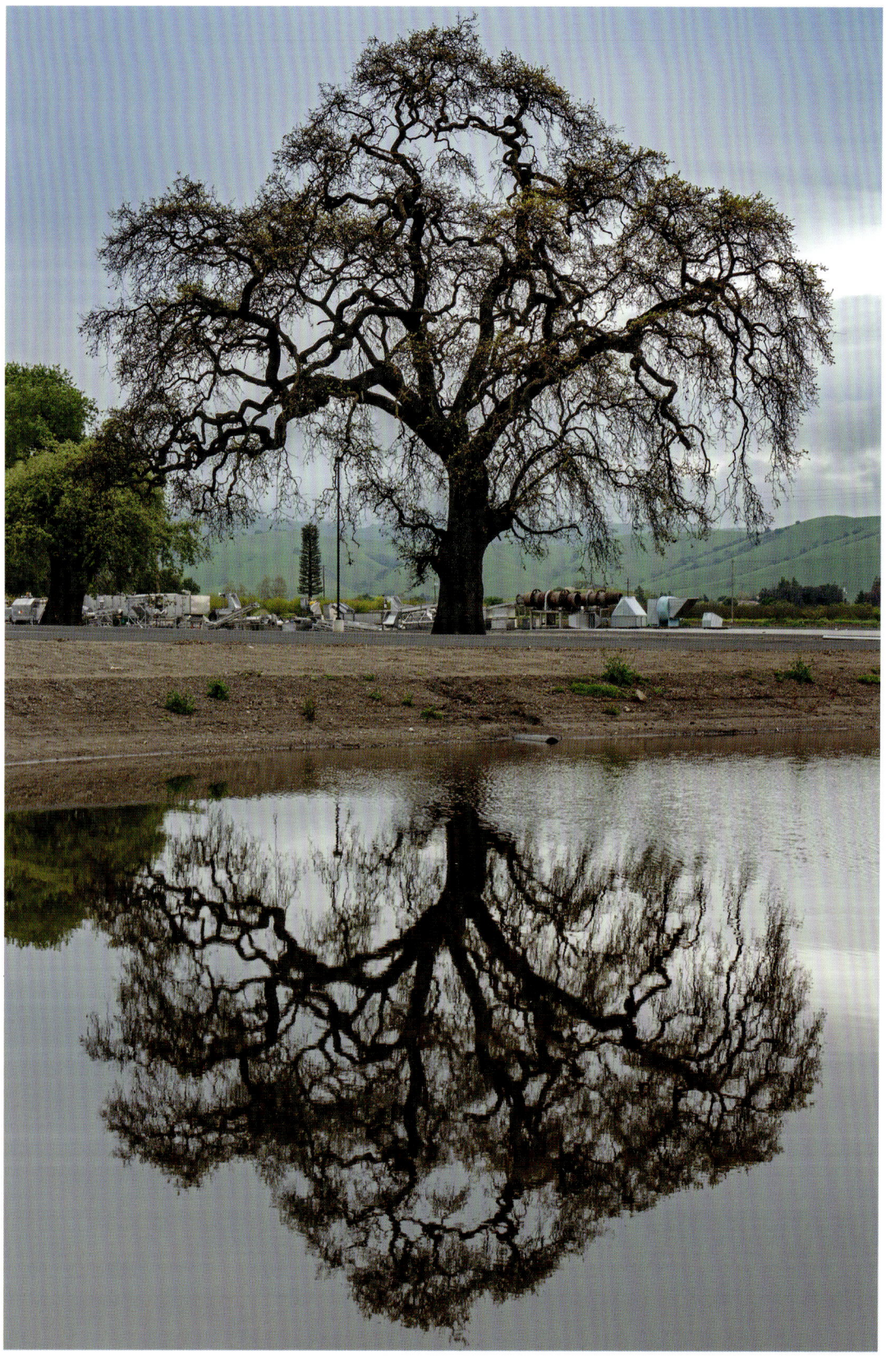

Oak Reflection, Hollister, CA – 2017

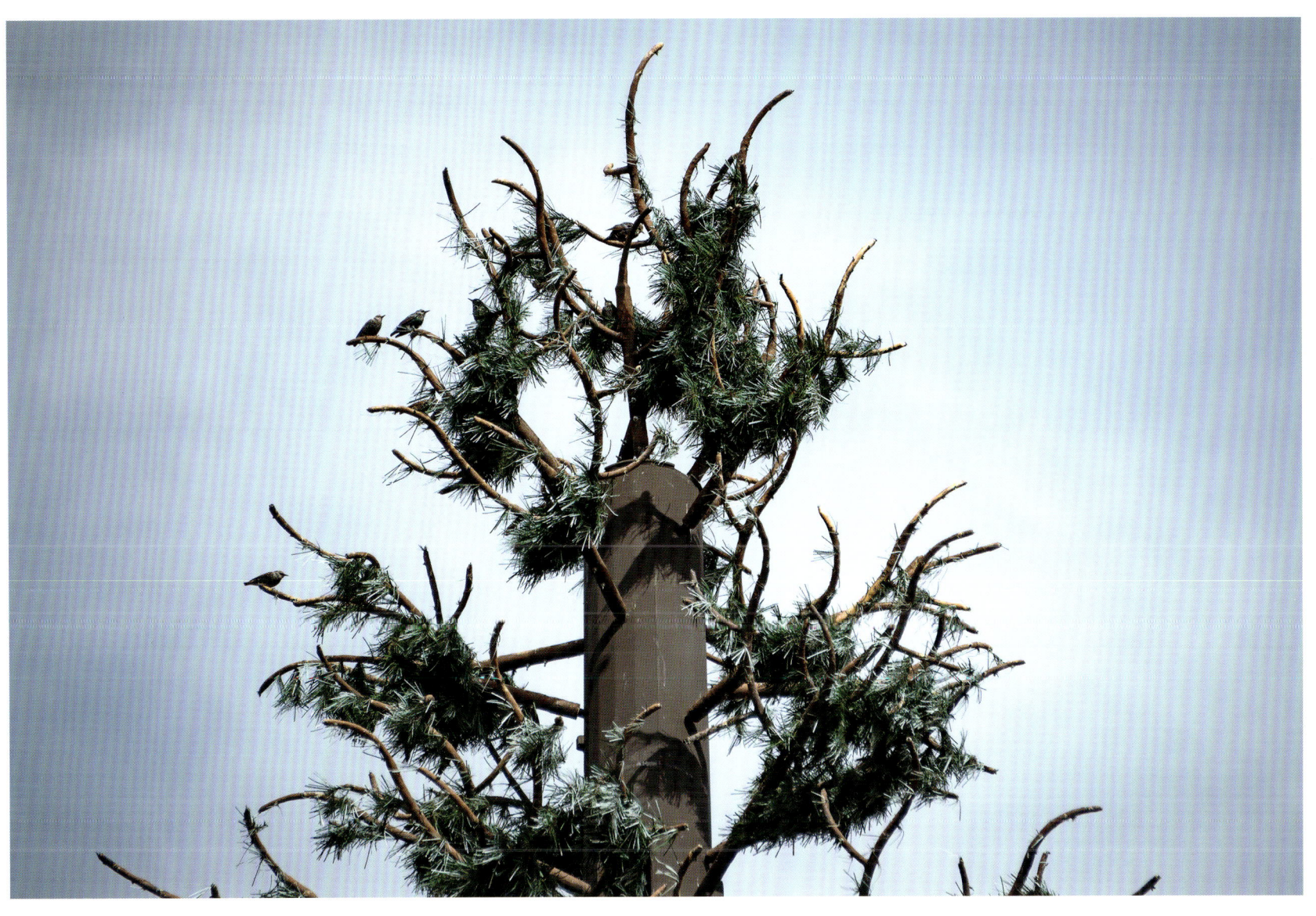

Avian Visitors, Santa Fe, NM – 2017

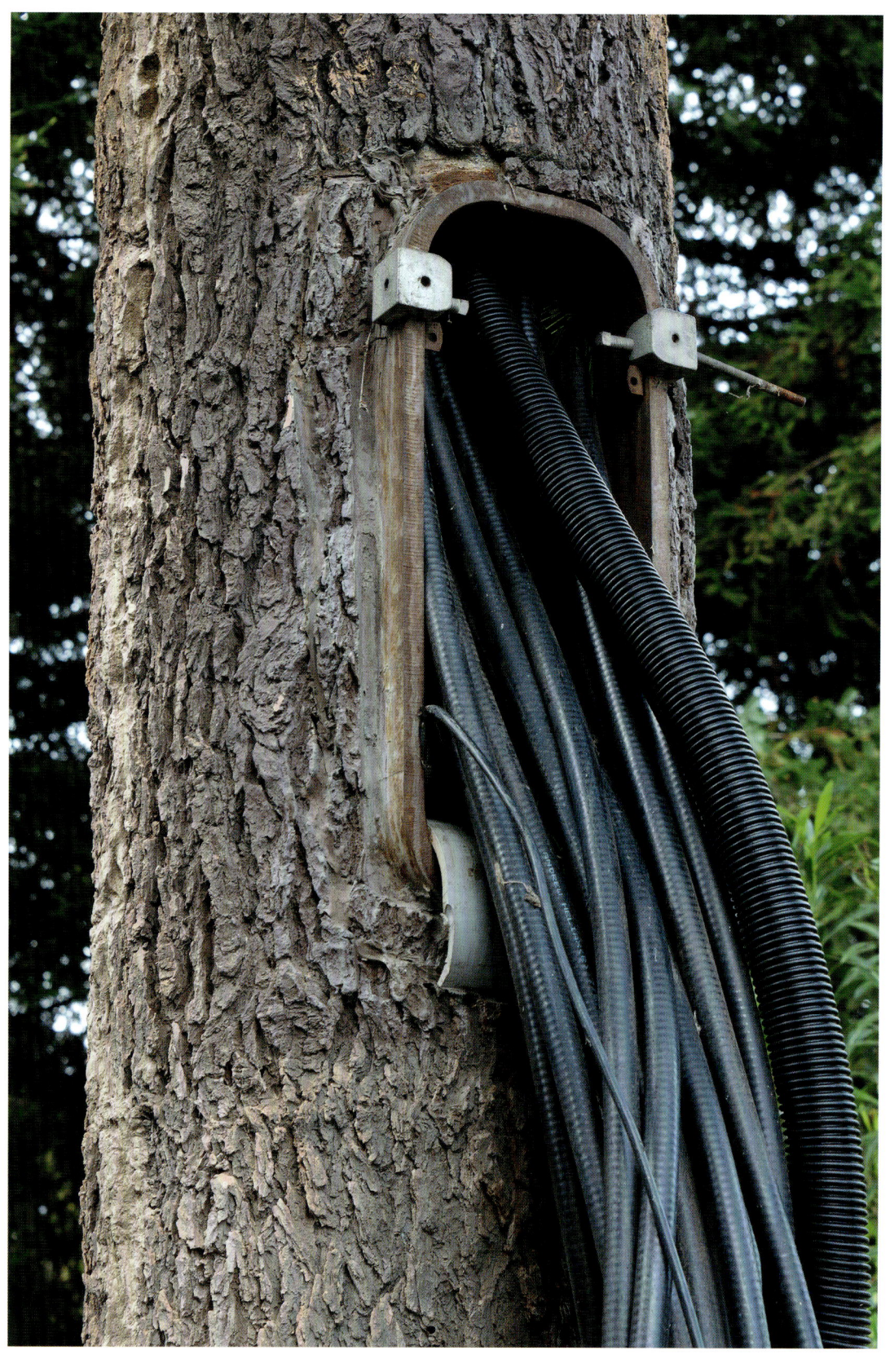

Hurling Cable, San Lorenzo, CA – 2017

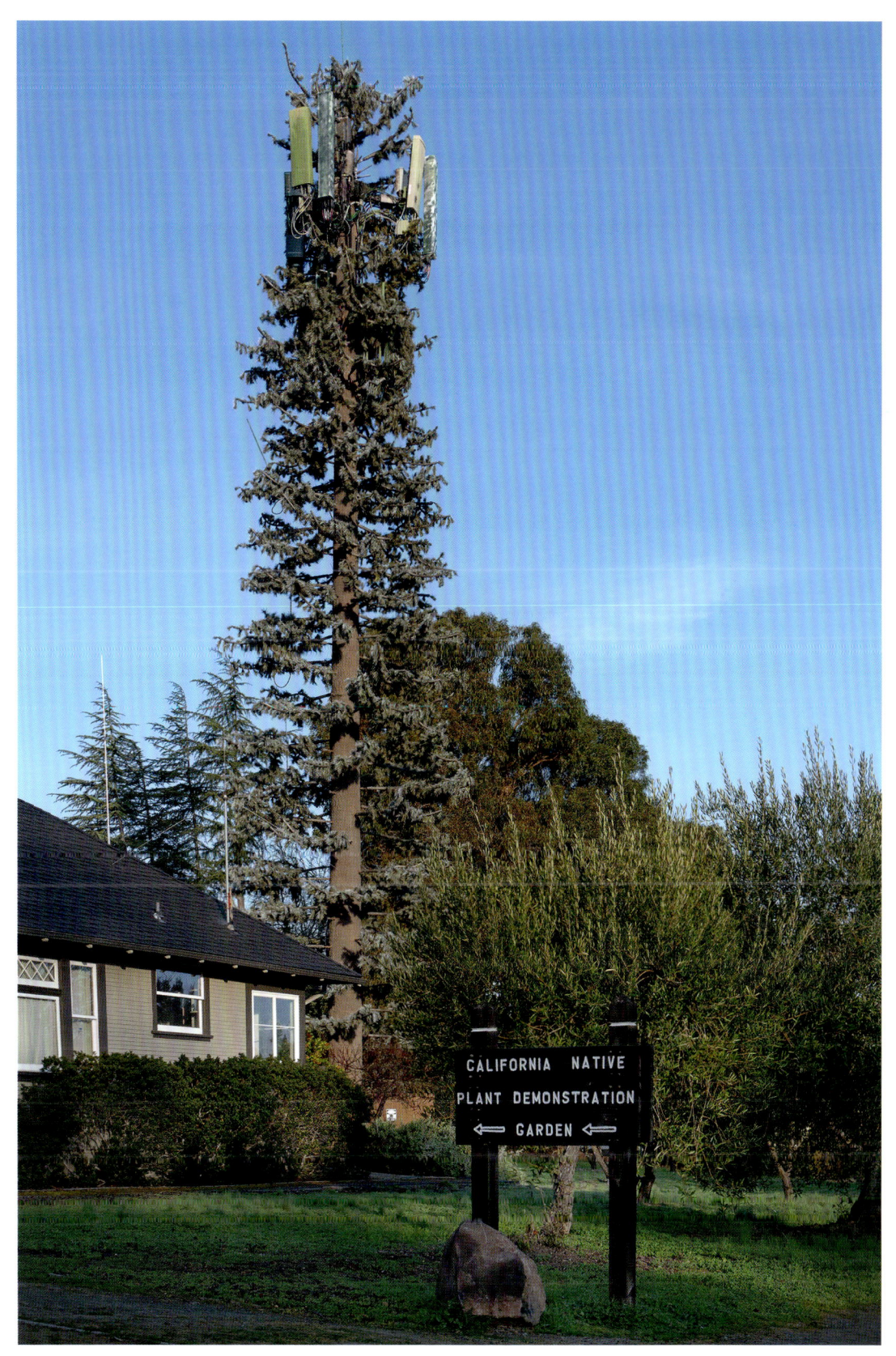

California Native Plant, Los Altos Hills, CA – 2020

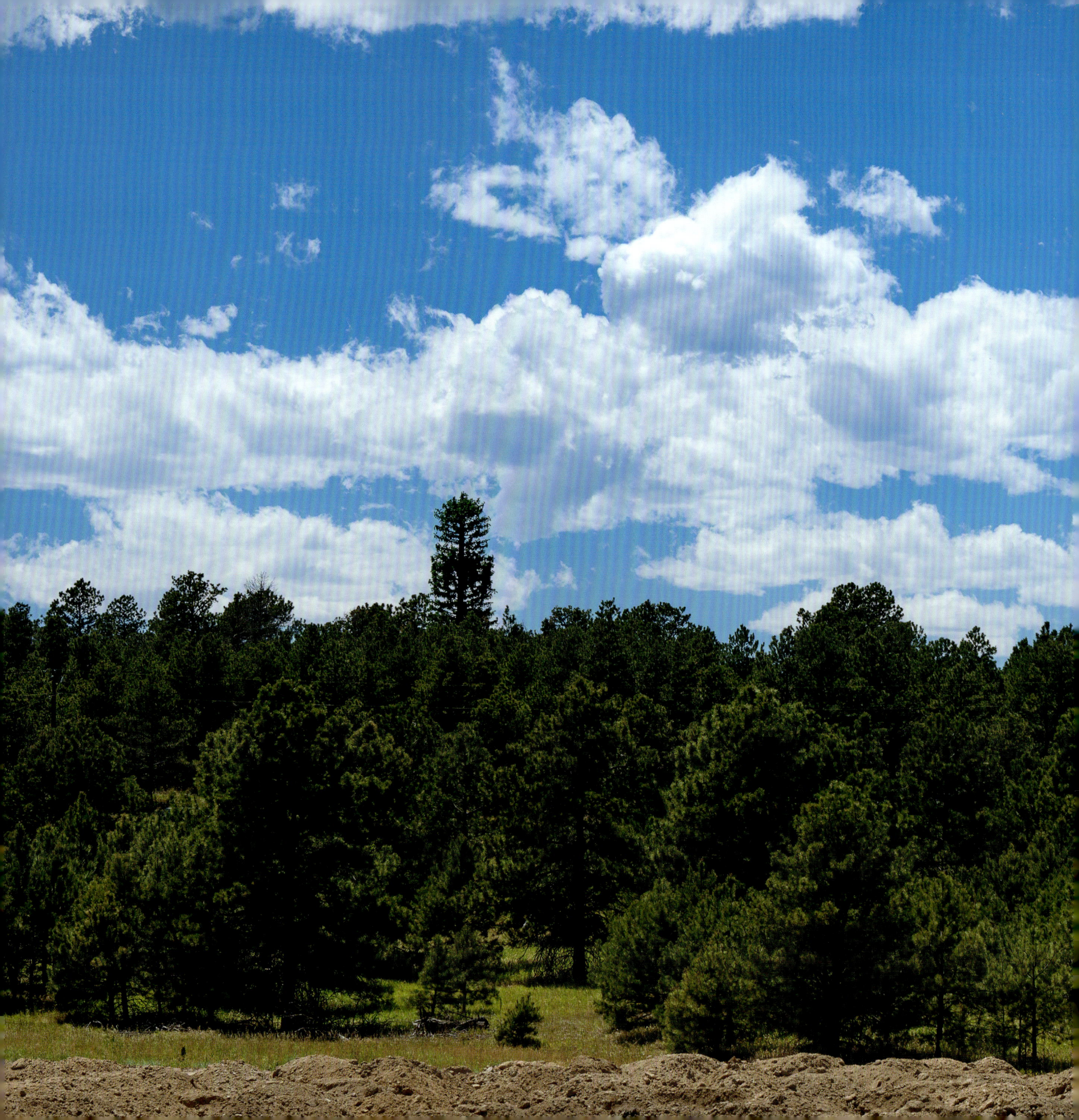

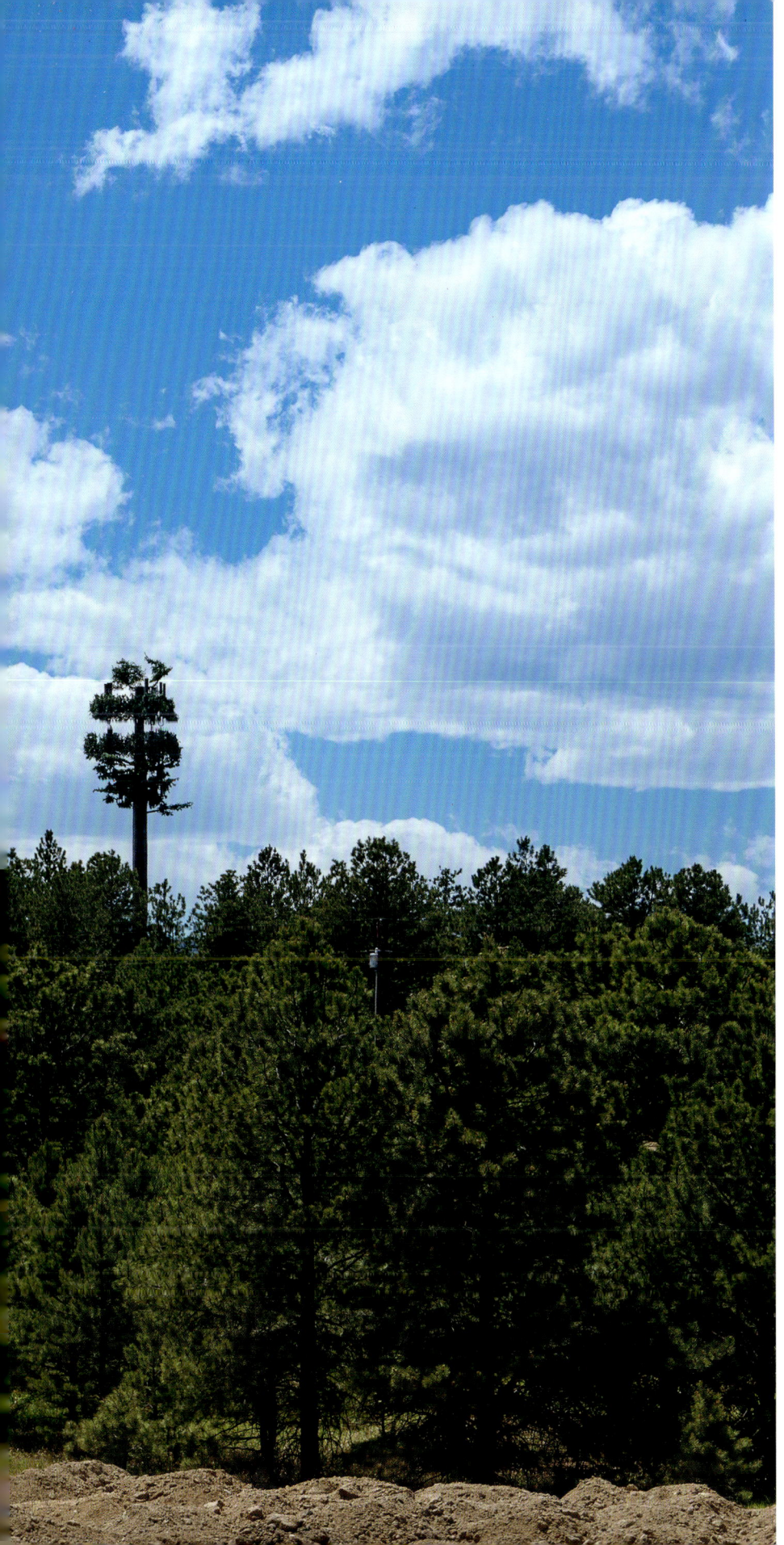

Frankenpines, Monument, CO – 2018

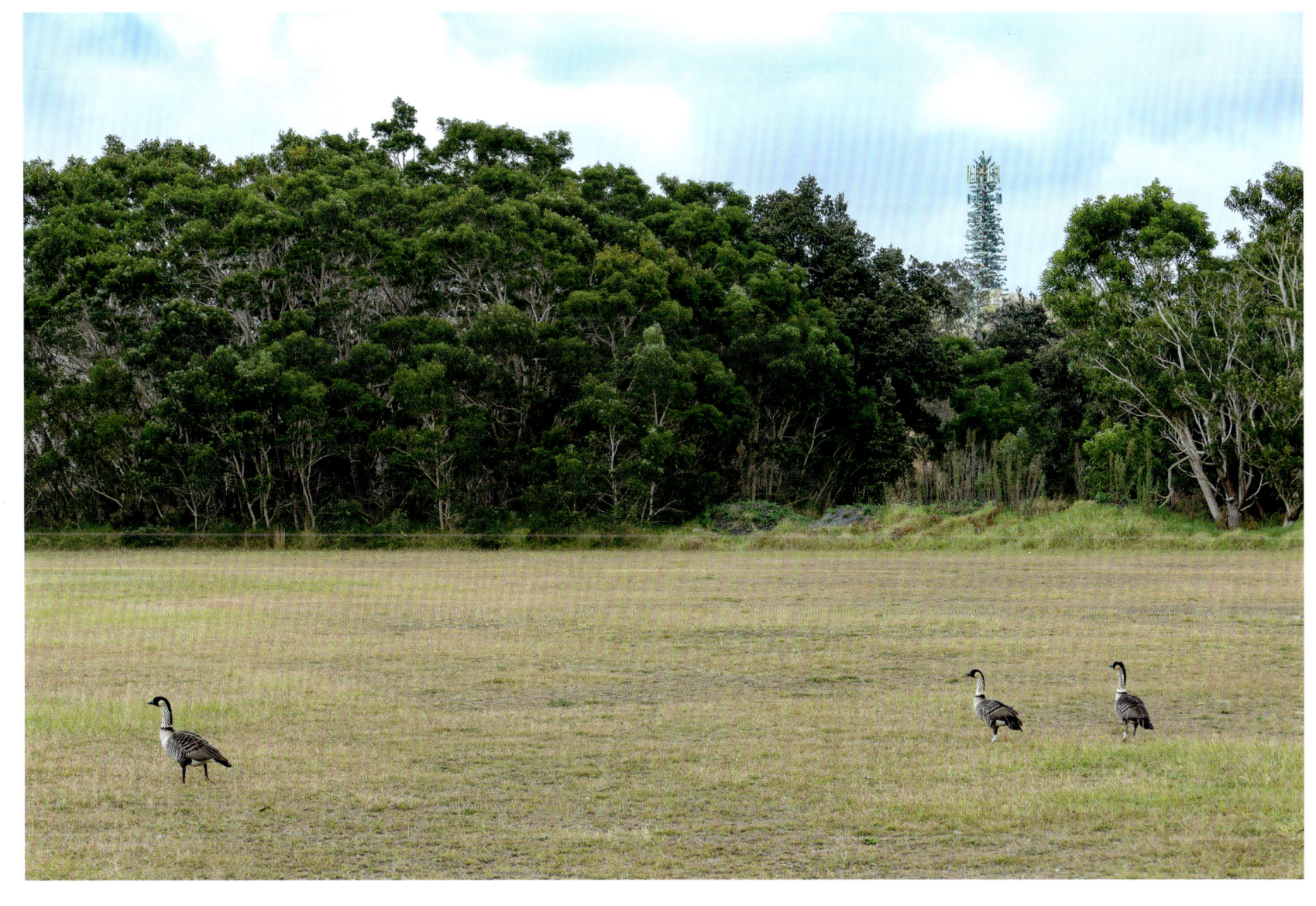

Nēnē, Hawai'i Volcanoes National Park, Big Island, HI – 2015

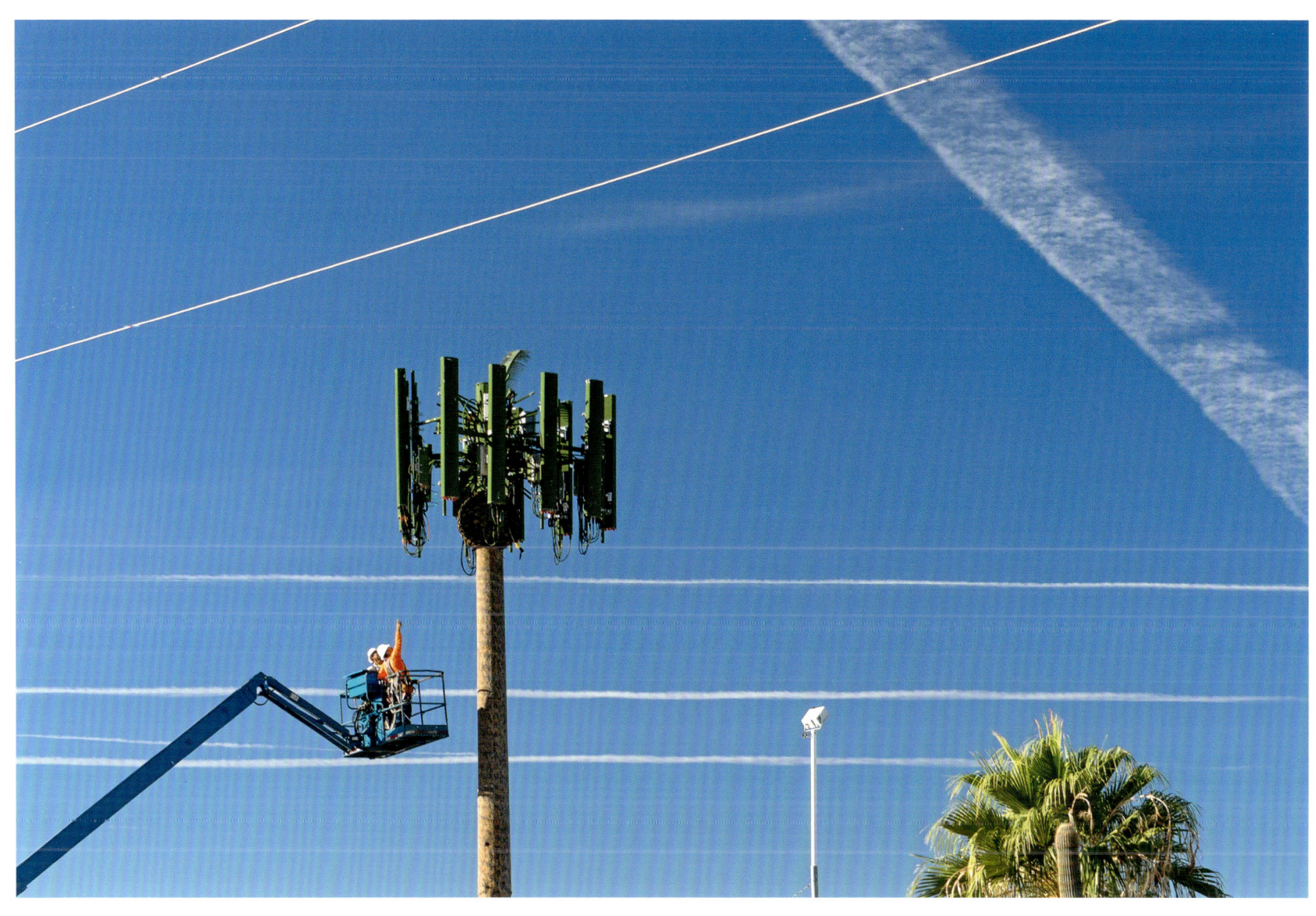

Contrails and Repairs, Phoenix, AZ – 2016

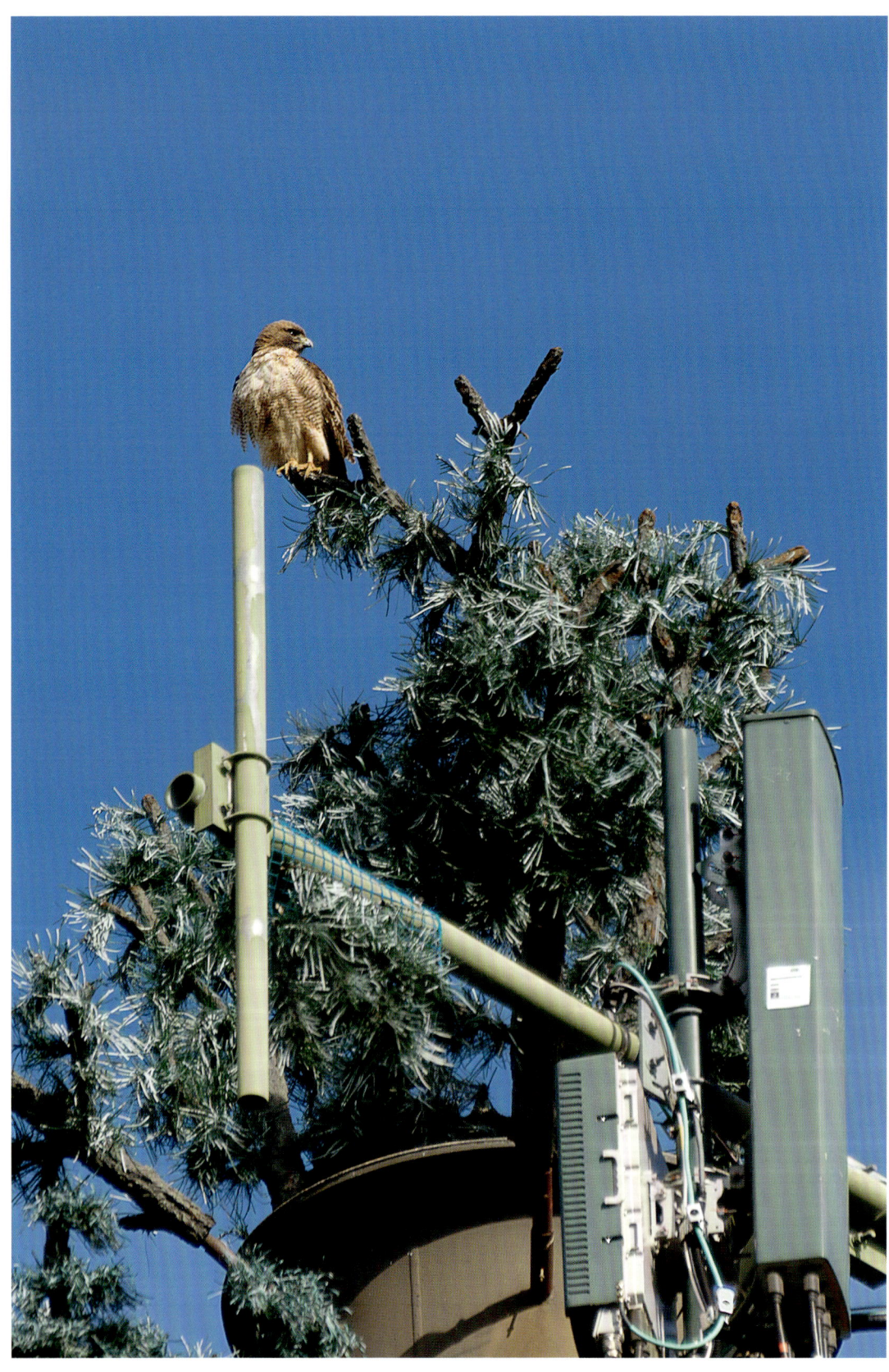

Falcon Perch, Calimesa, CA – 2017

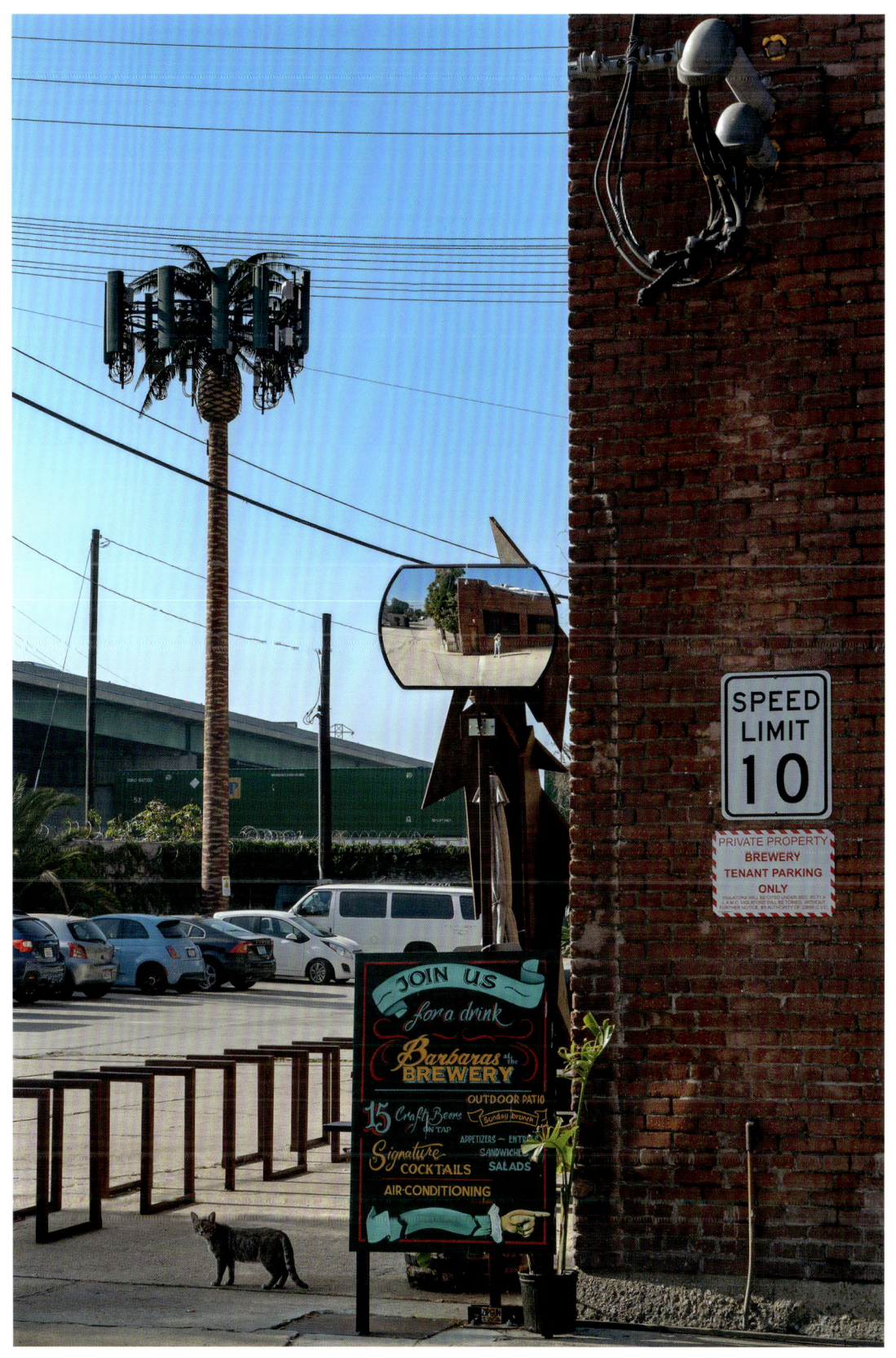

Self-Portrait with Cat, Los Angeles, CA – 2016

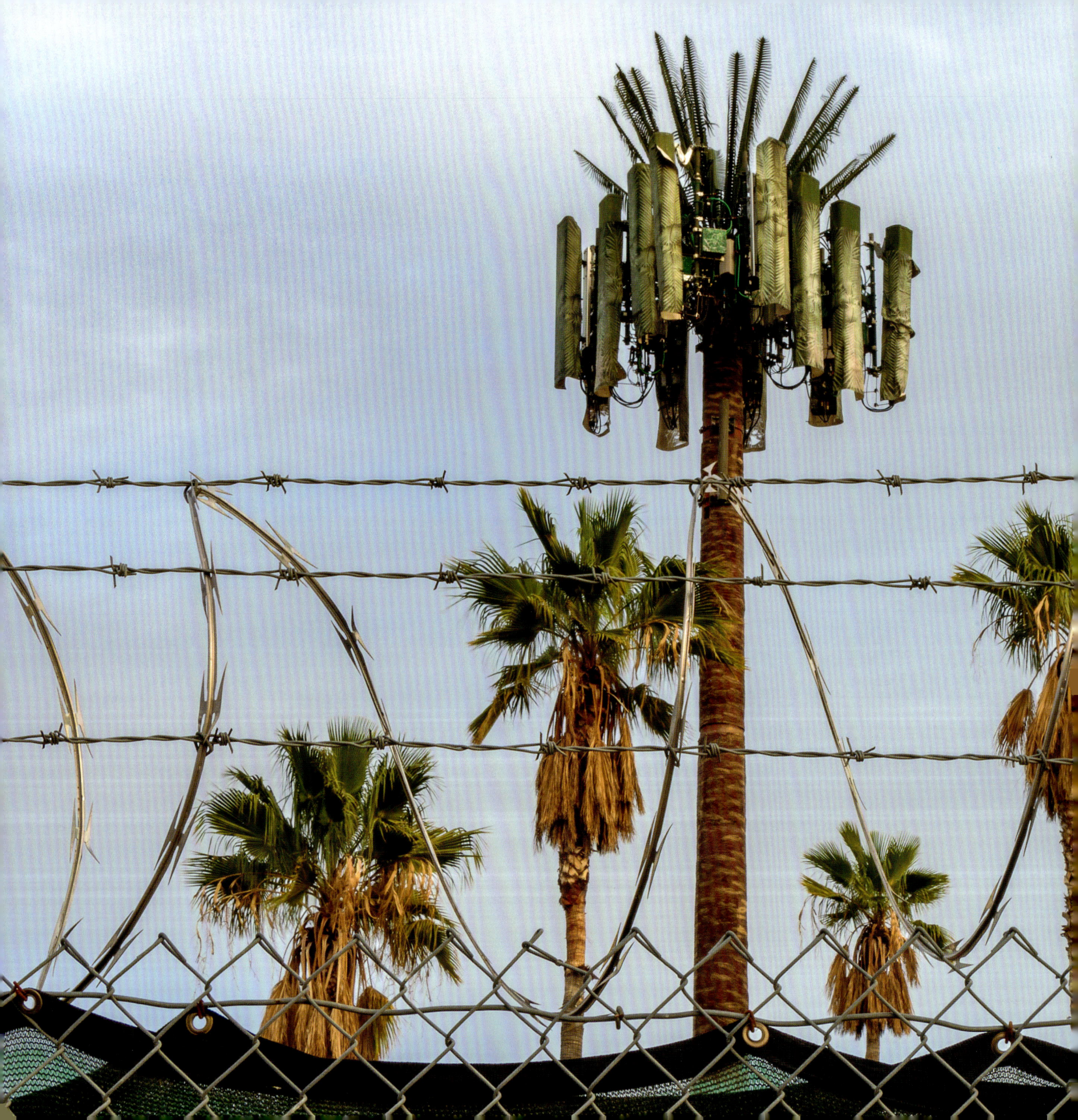

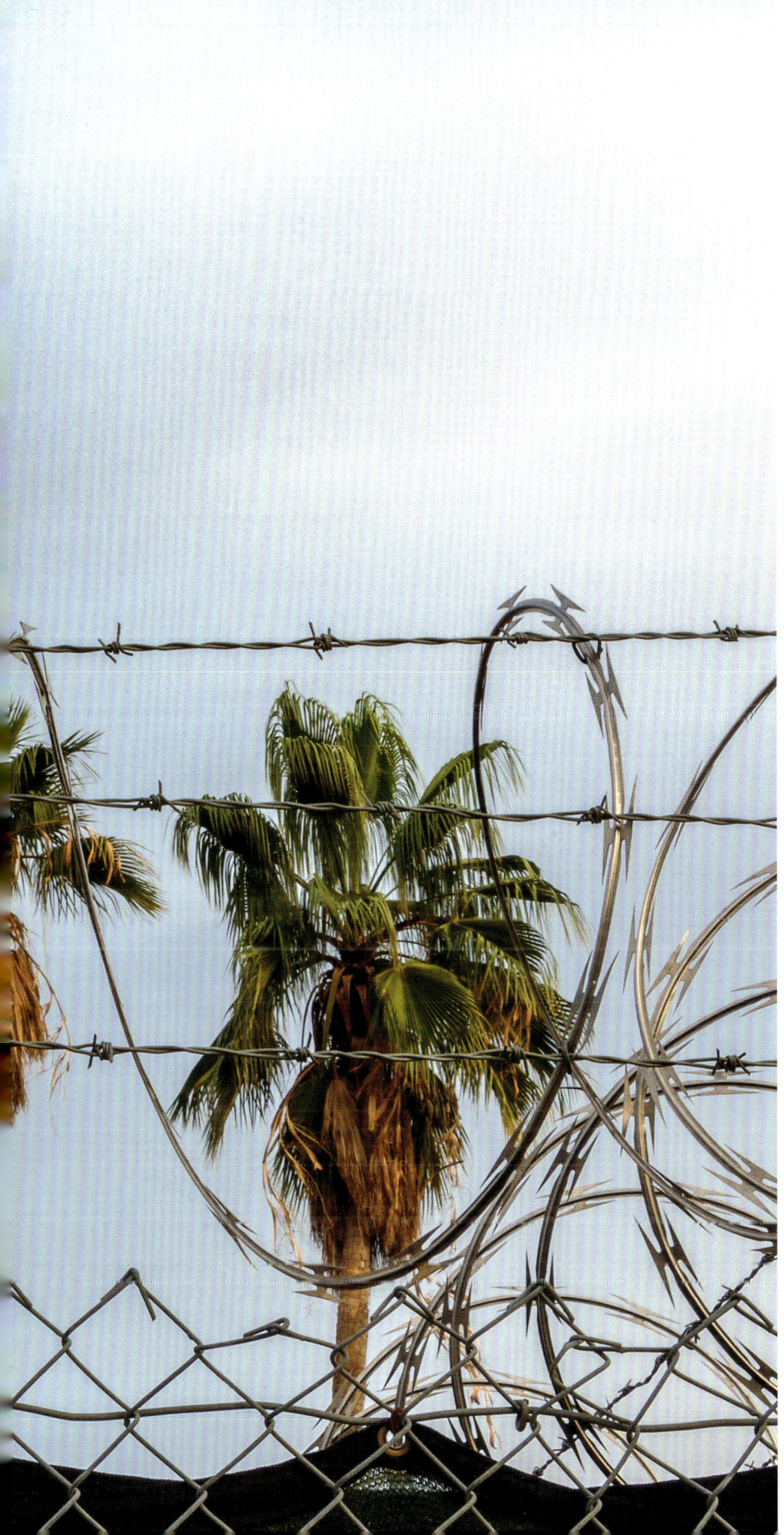

Barbed Wire, San Bernardino, CA – 2017

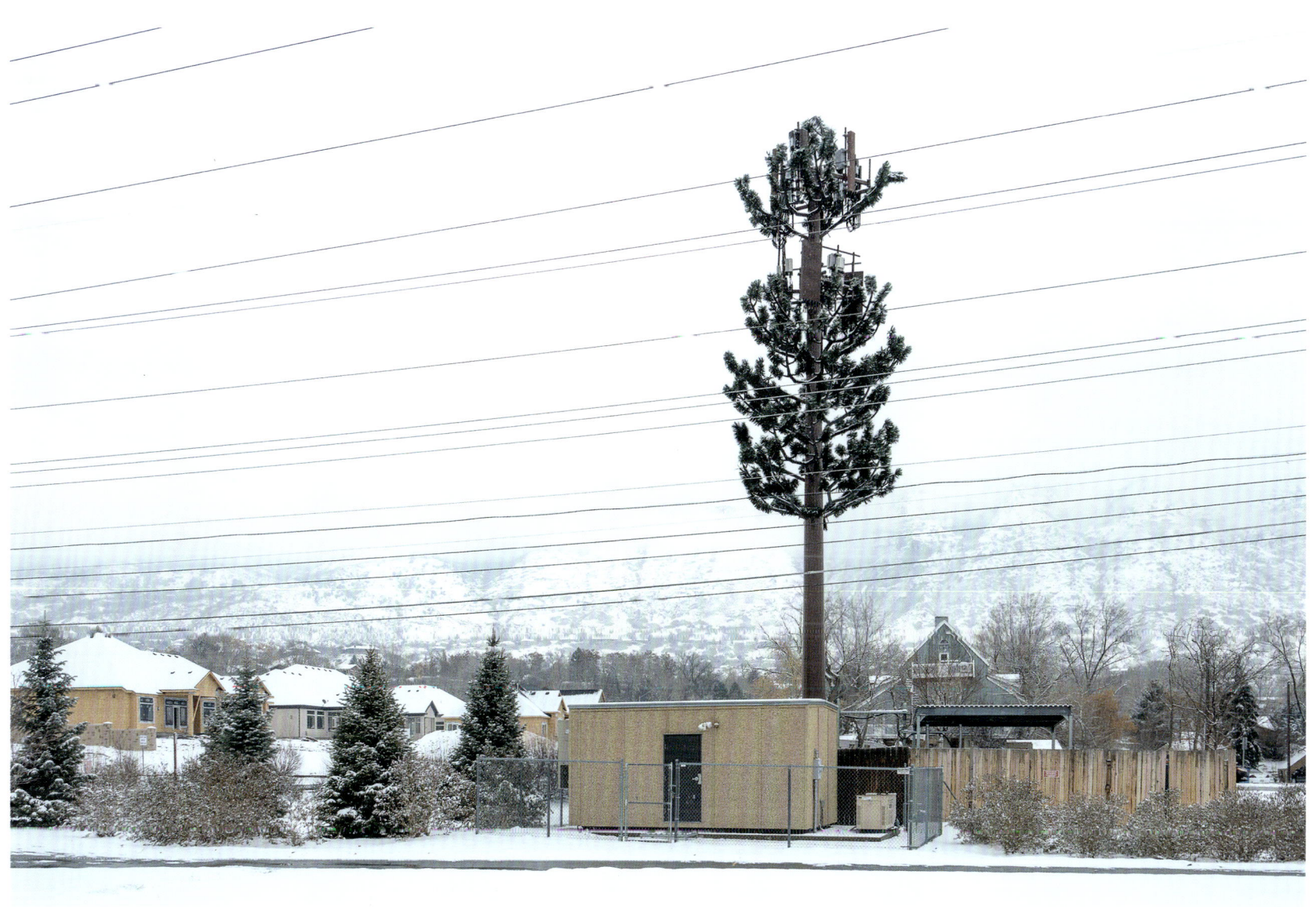

Snowfall, Provo, UT – 2018

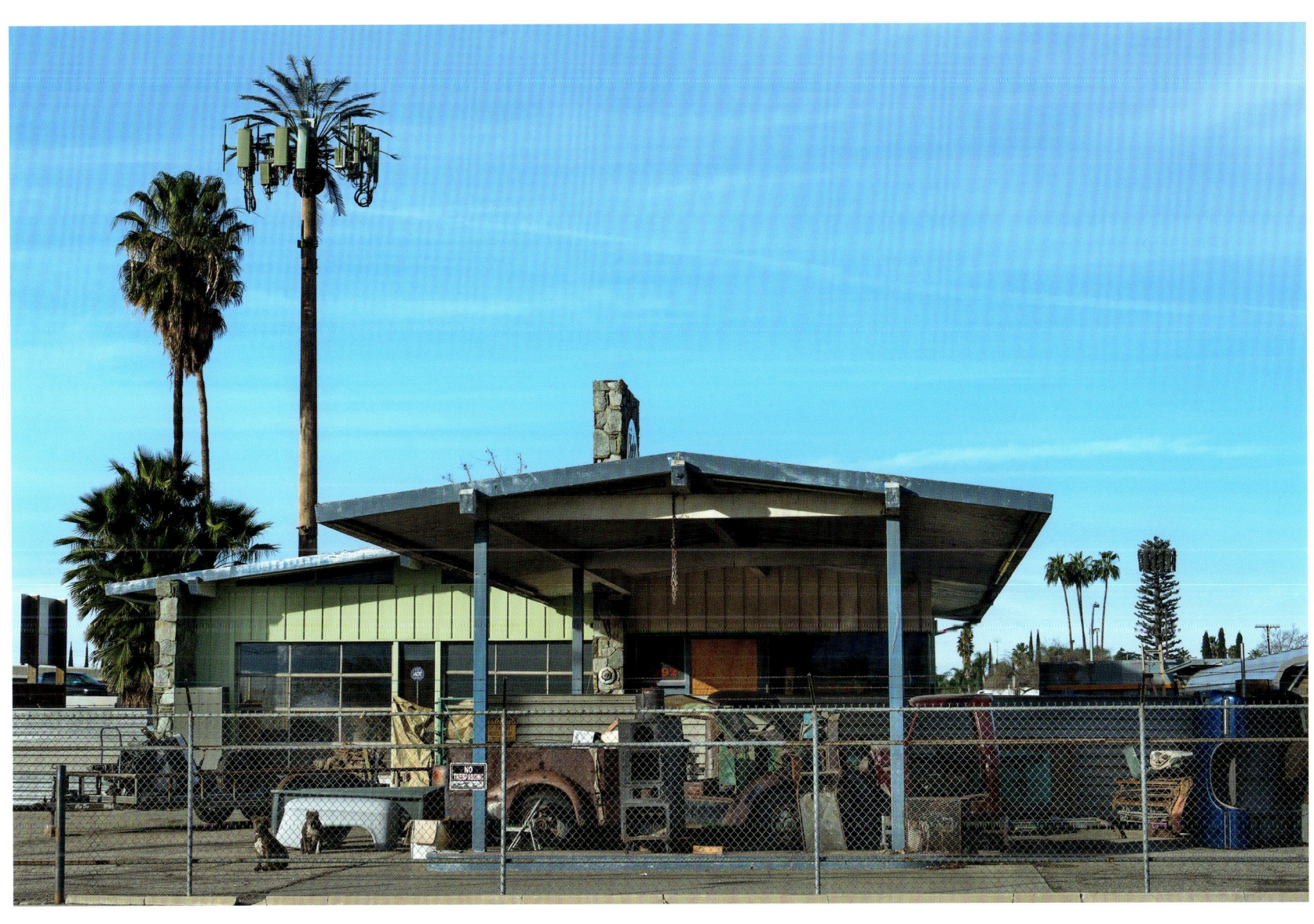

Junkyard Dogs, San Bernardino, CA – 2017

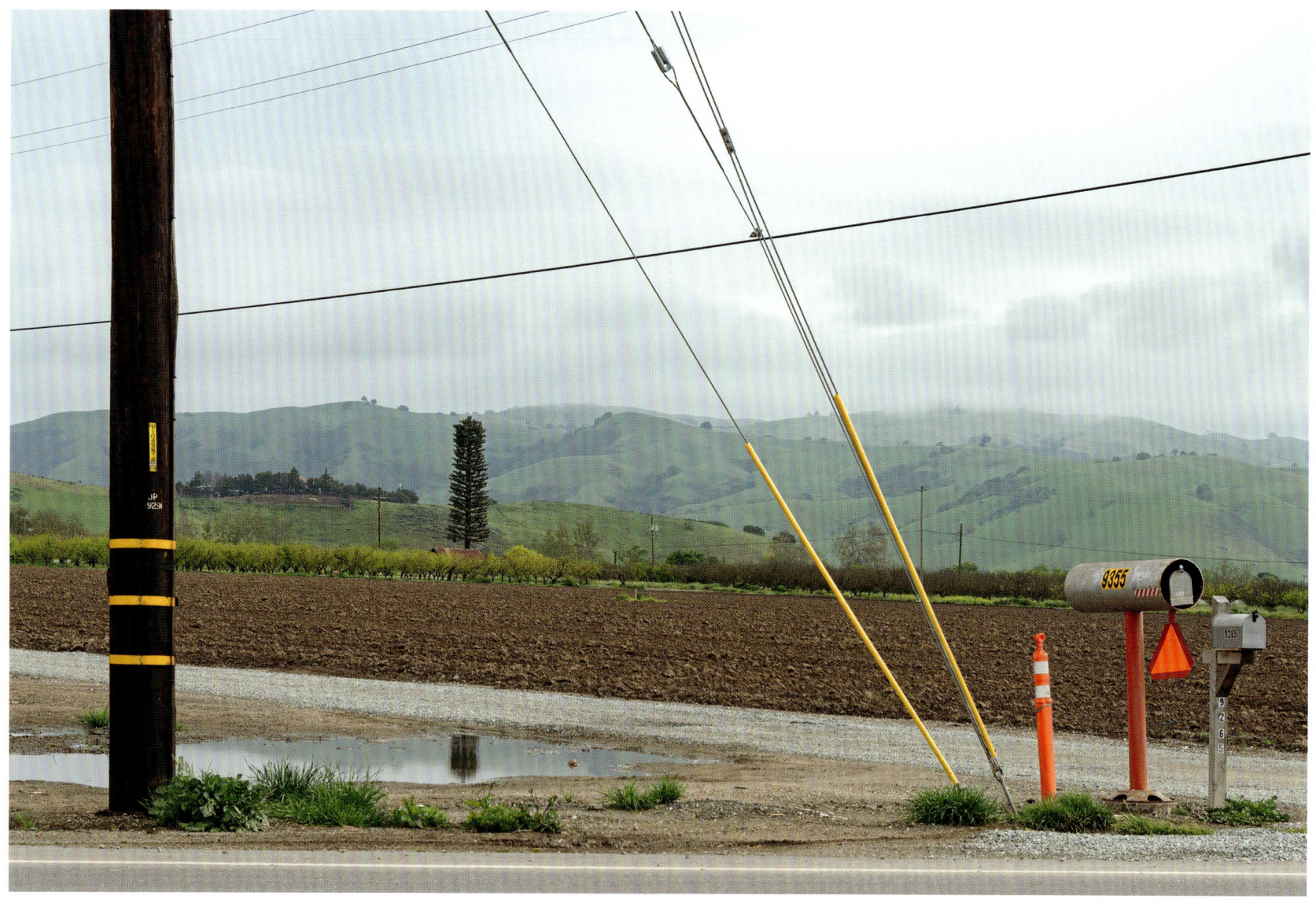

Communication Lines, Hollister, CA – 2017

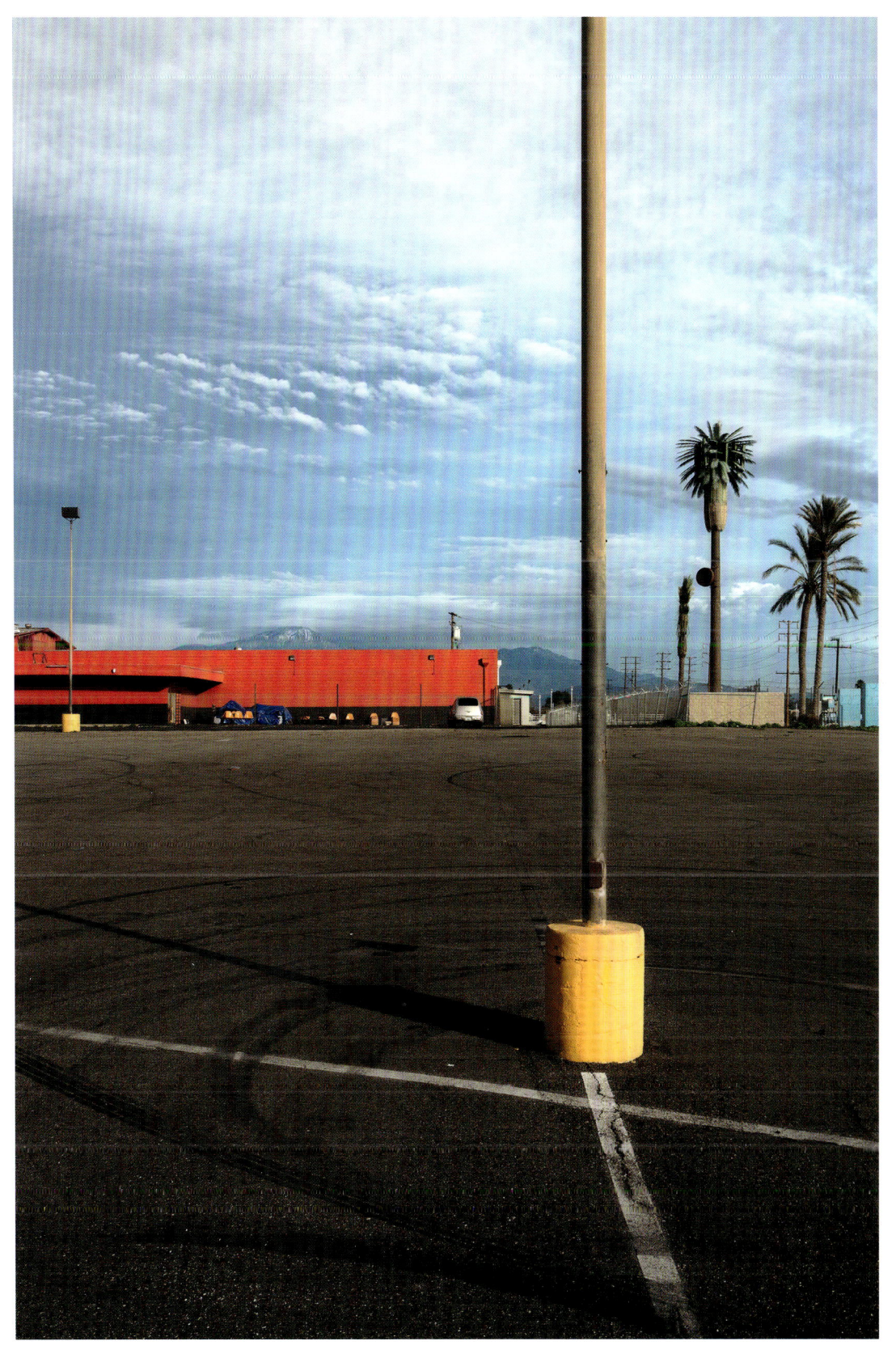

Between the Bowling Alley and the Sewer
Treatment Plant, San Bernardino, CA – 2017

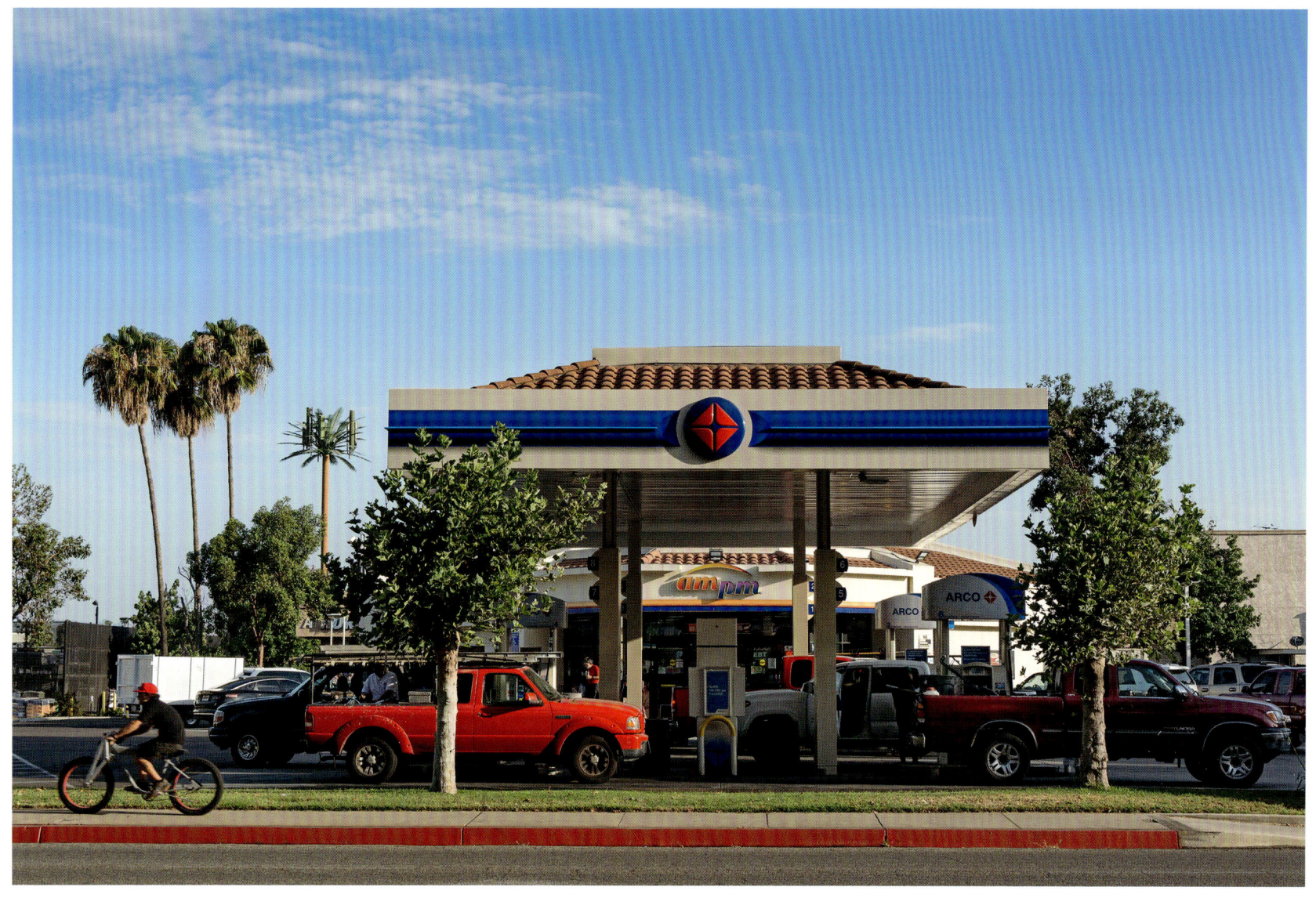

Morning Fill-Up, Escondido, CA – 2018

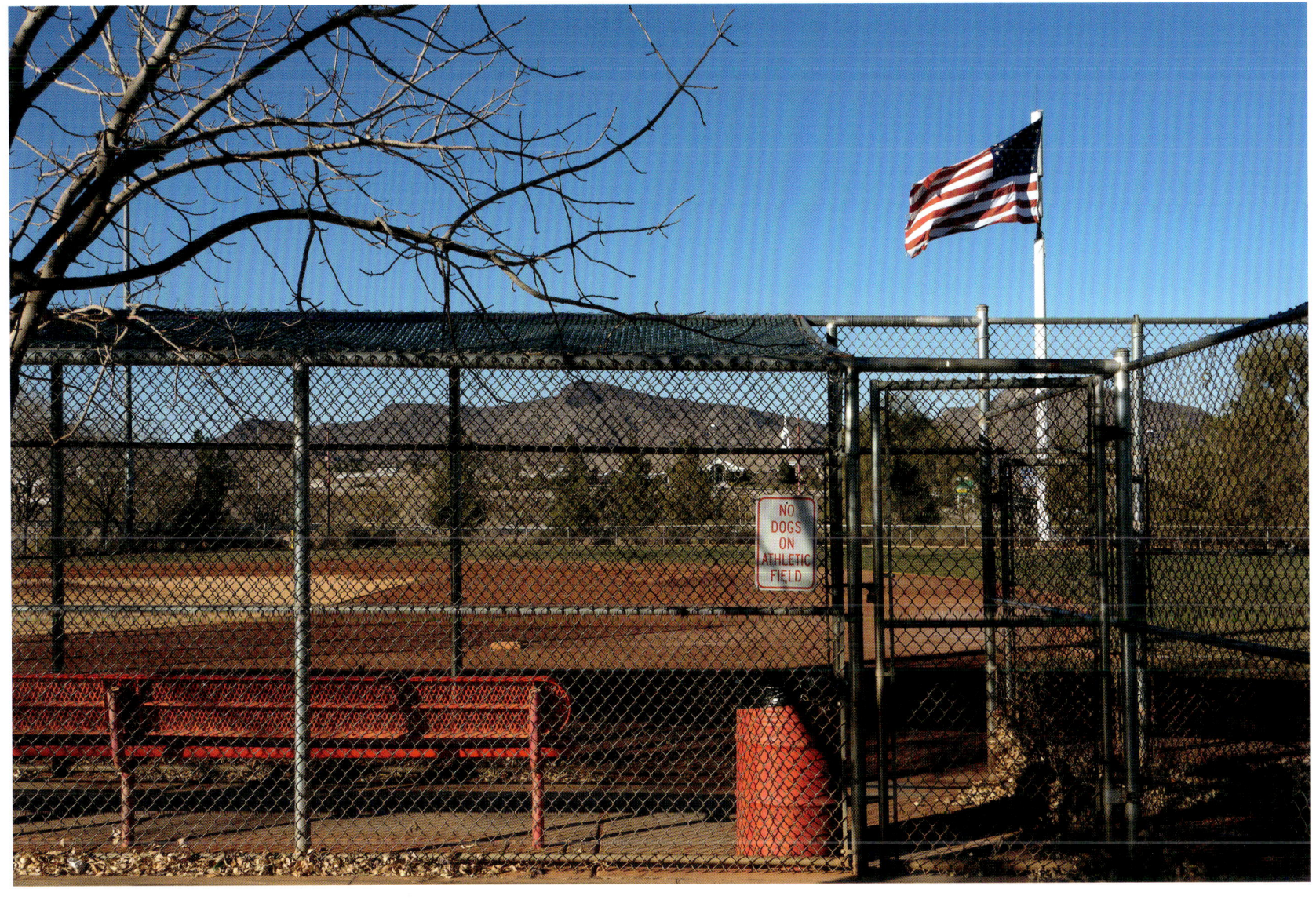

Little League Flagpole, Henderson, NV – 2019

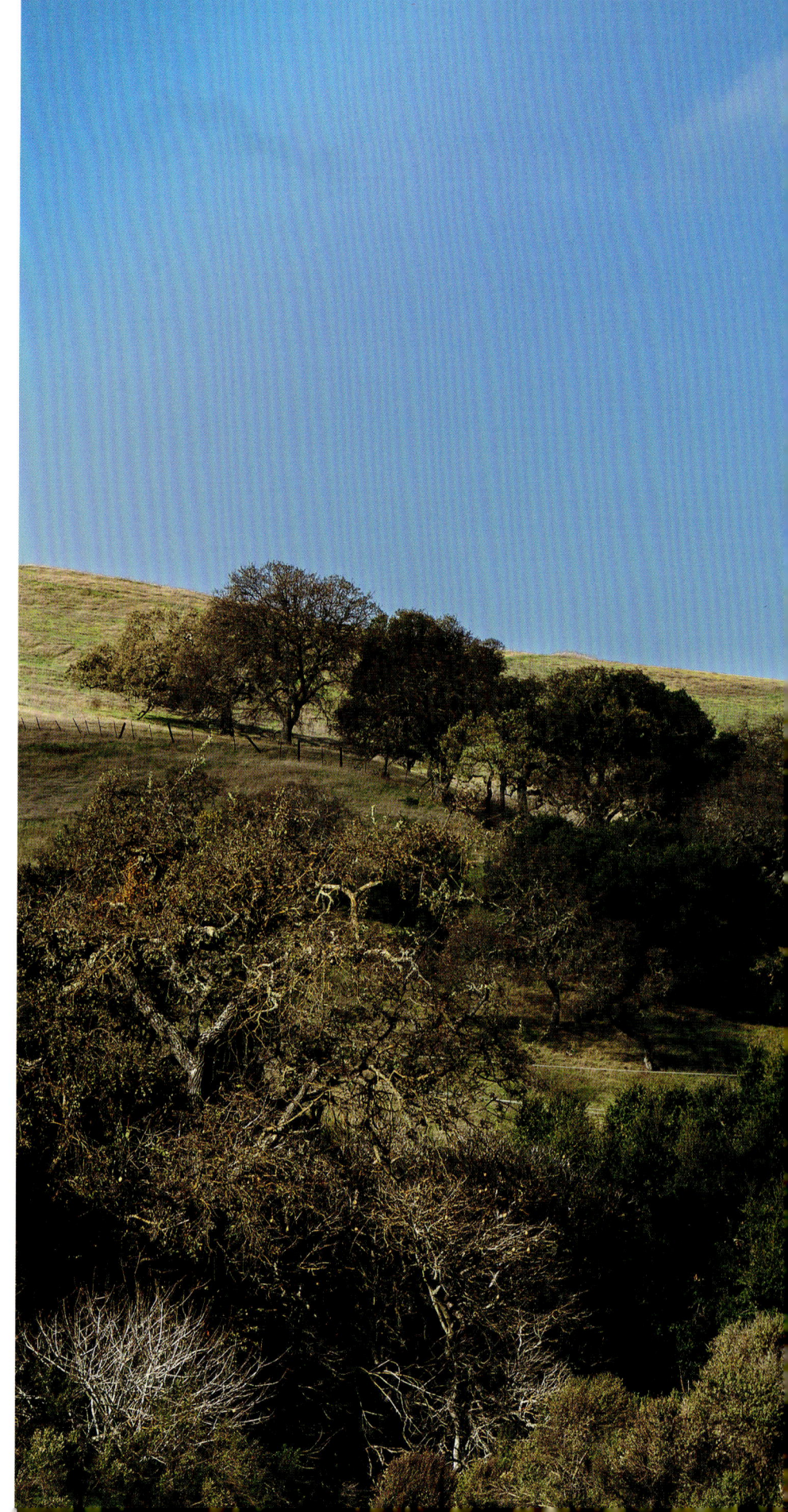

Stanford Rainbow, Palo Alto, CA – 2016

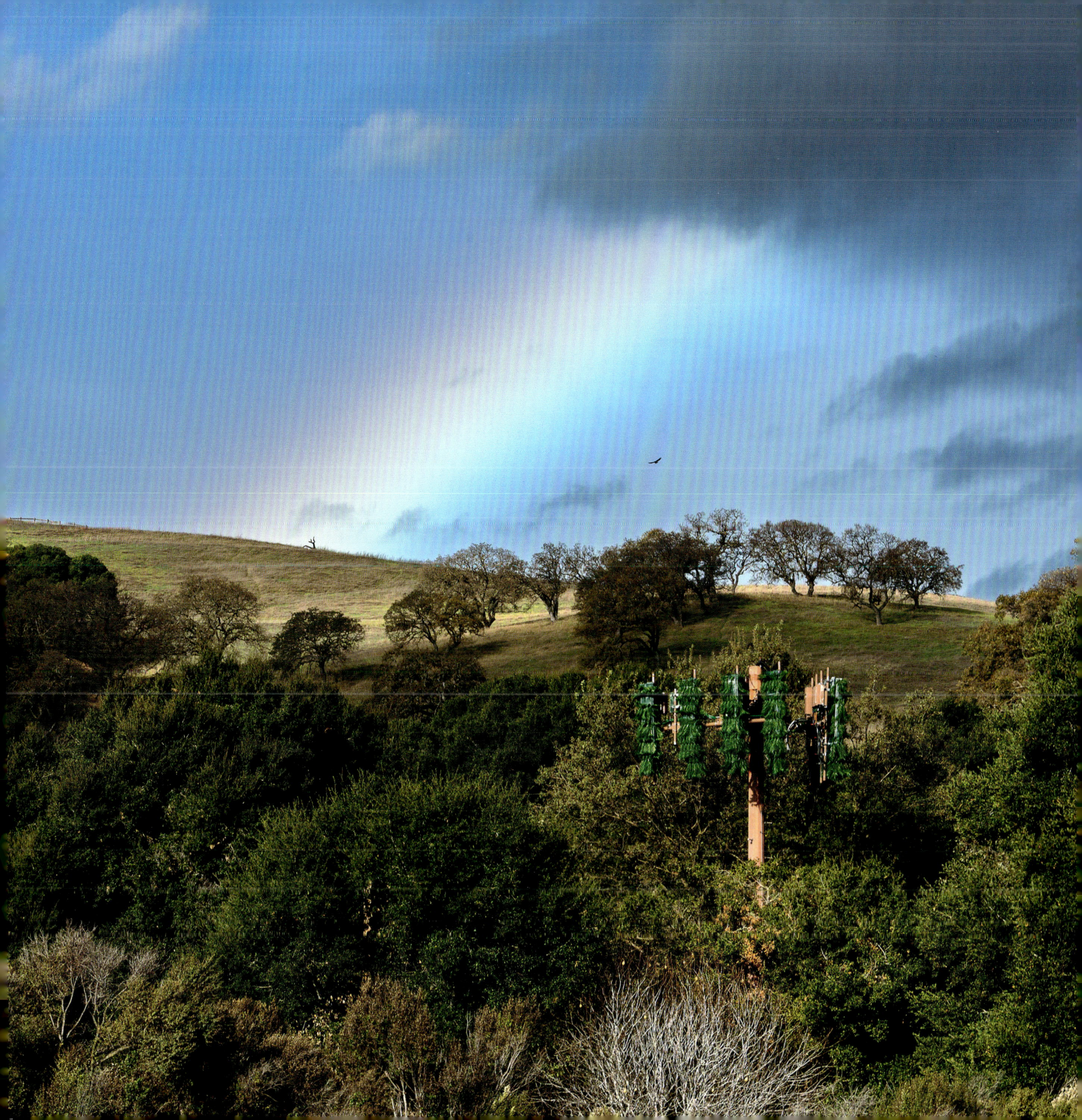

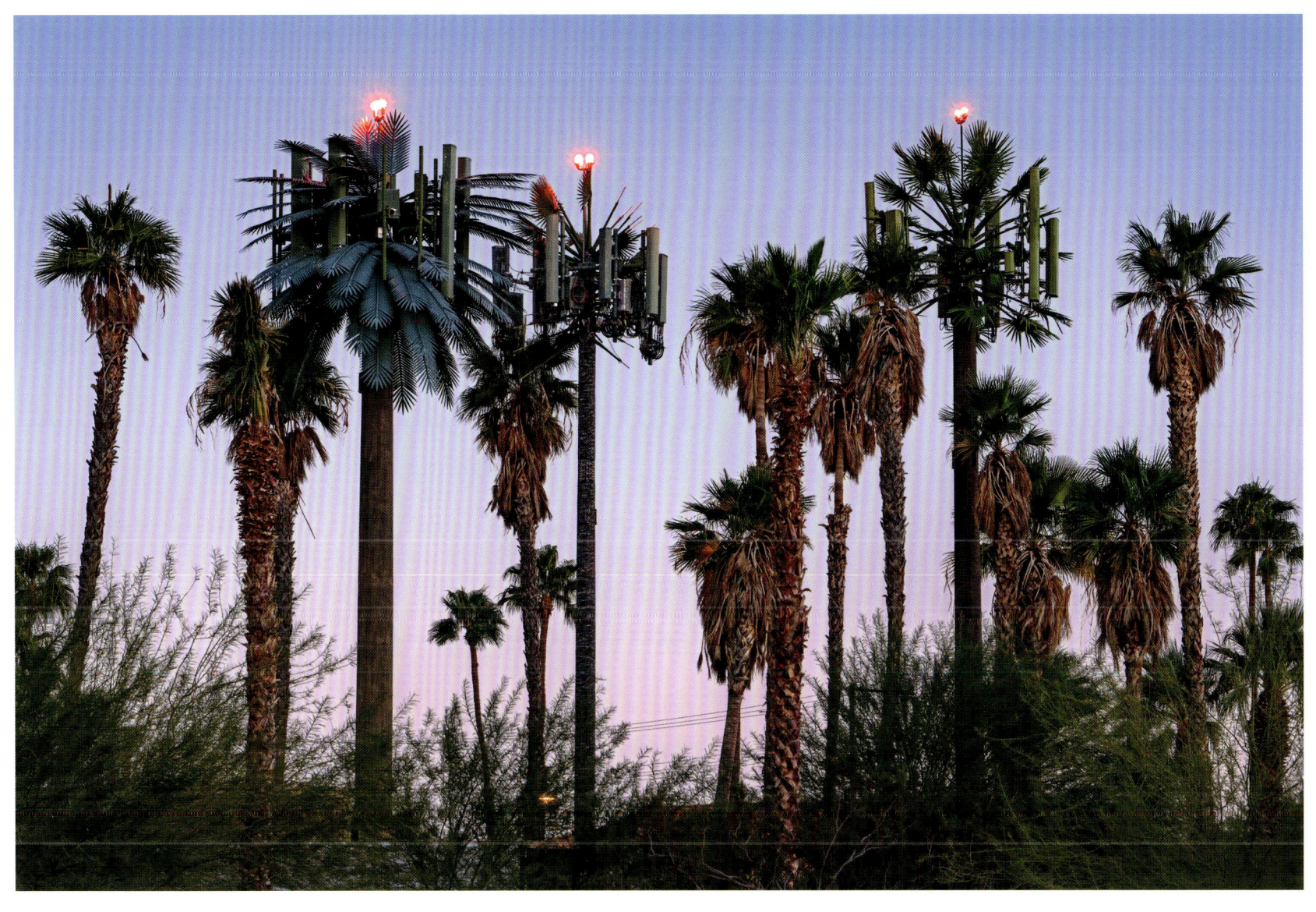

Airport Approach, Palm Springs, CA – 2019

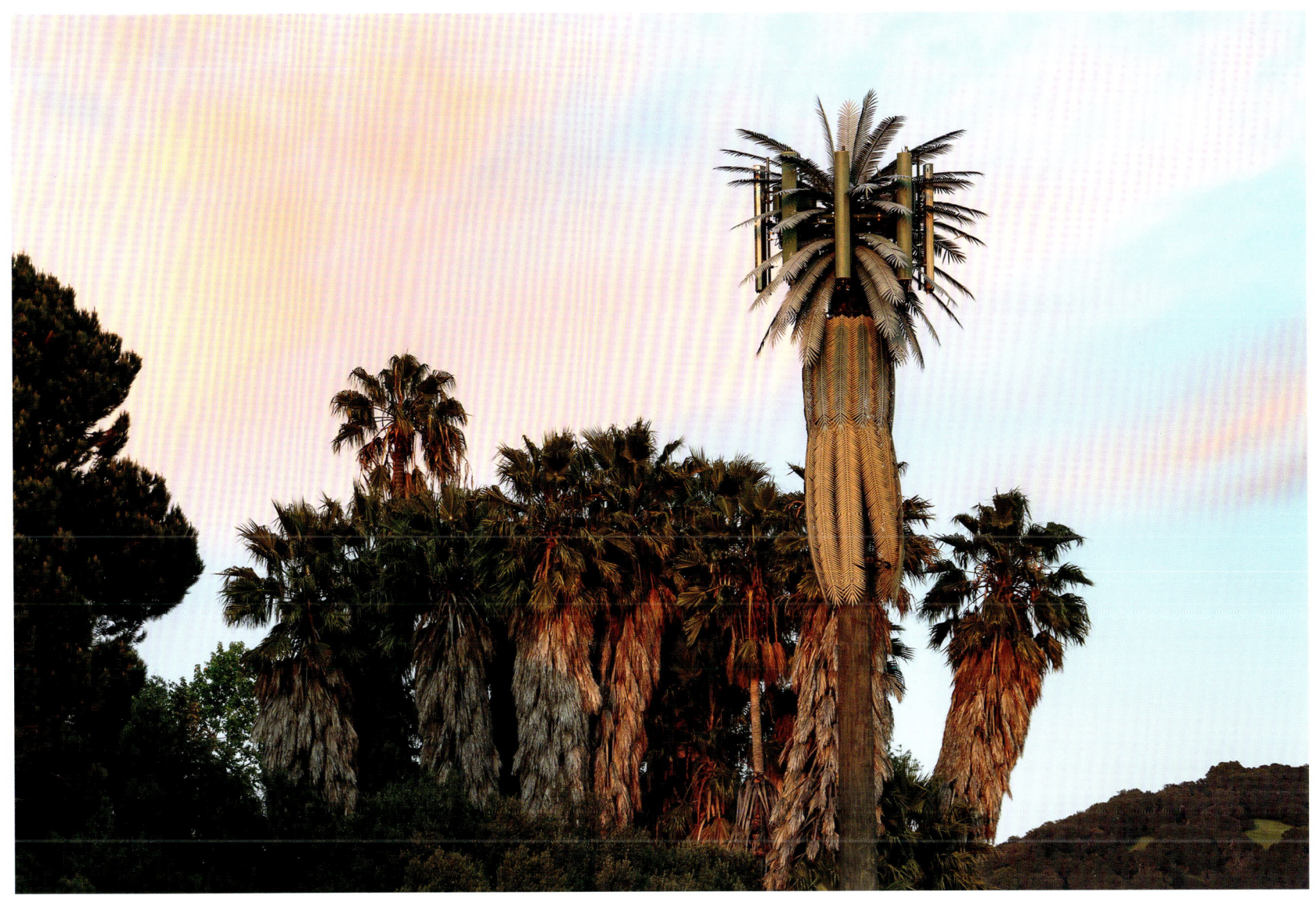

Skirted Palm, Fremont, CA – 2020

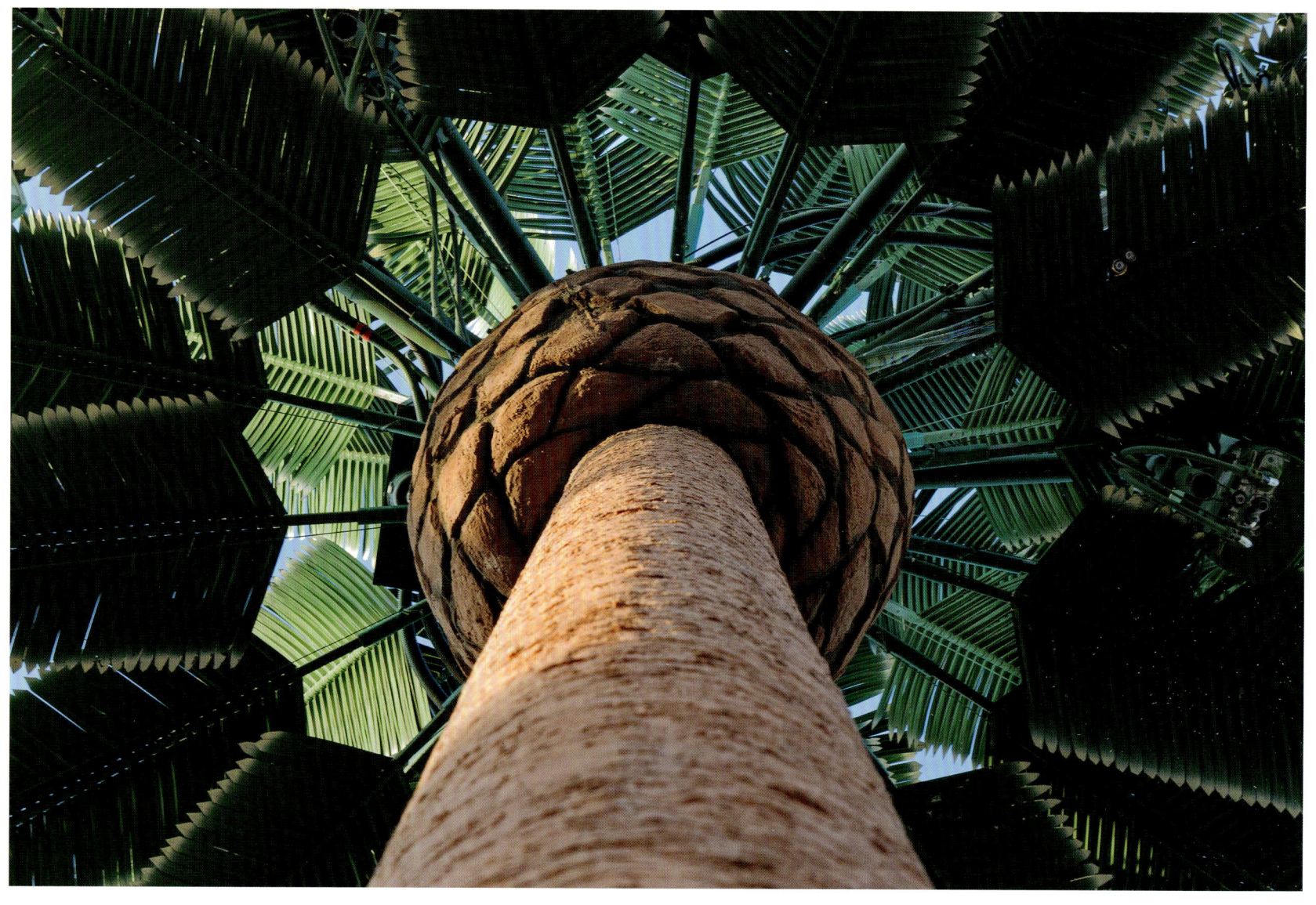

Looking Up, San Diego, CA – 2018

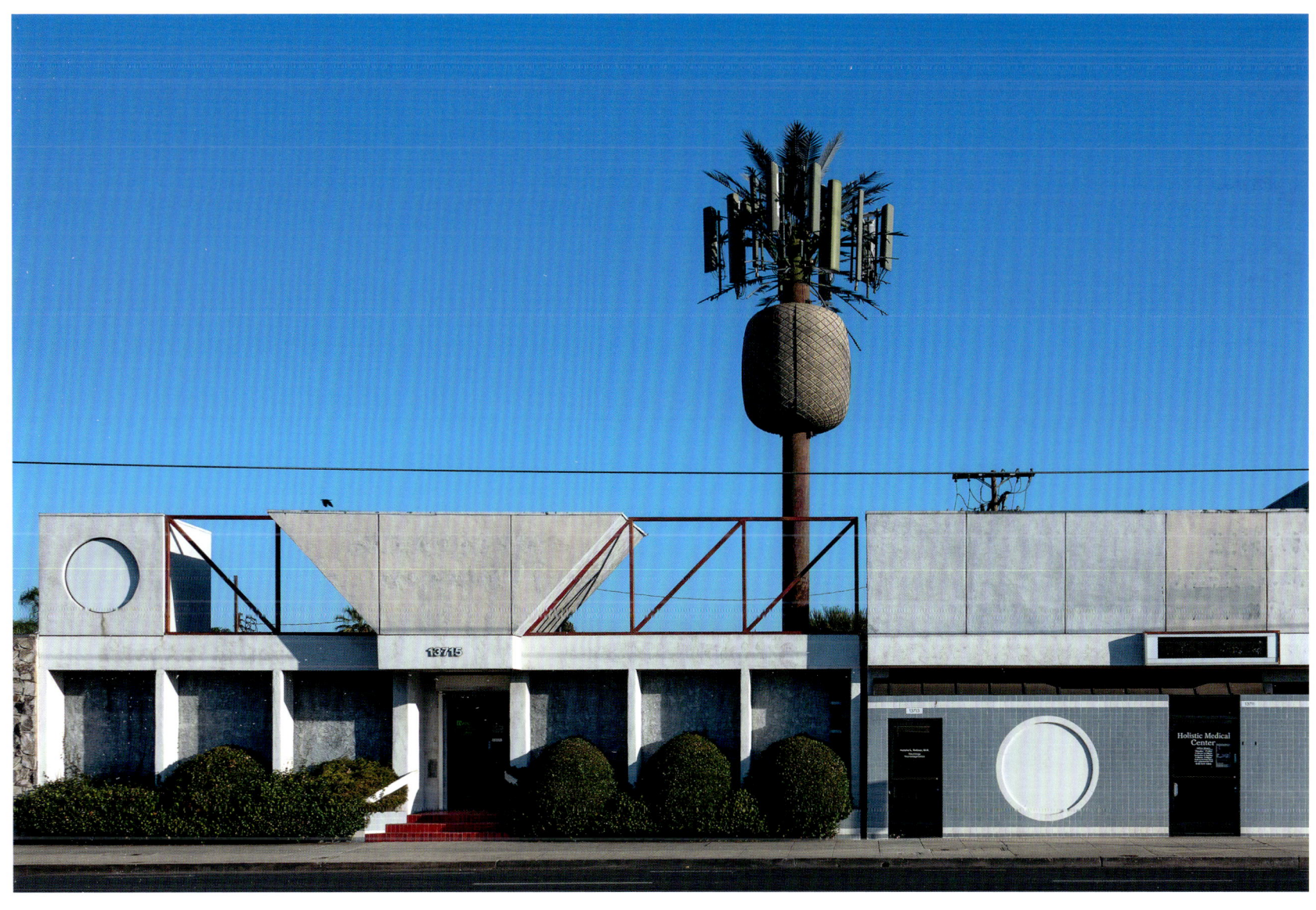

Spheroids, Van Nuys, CA – 2019

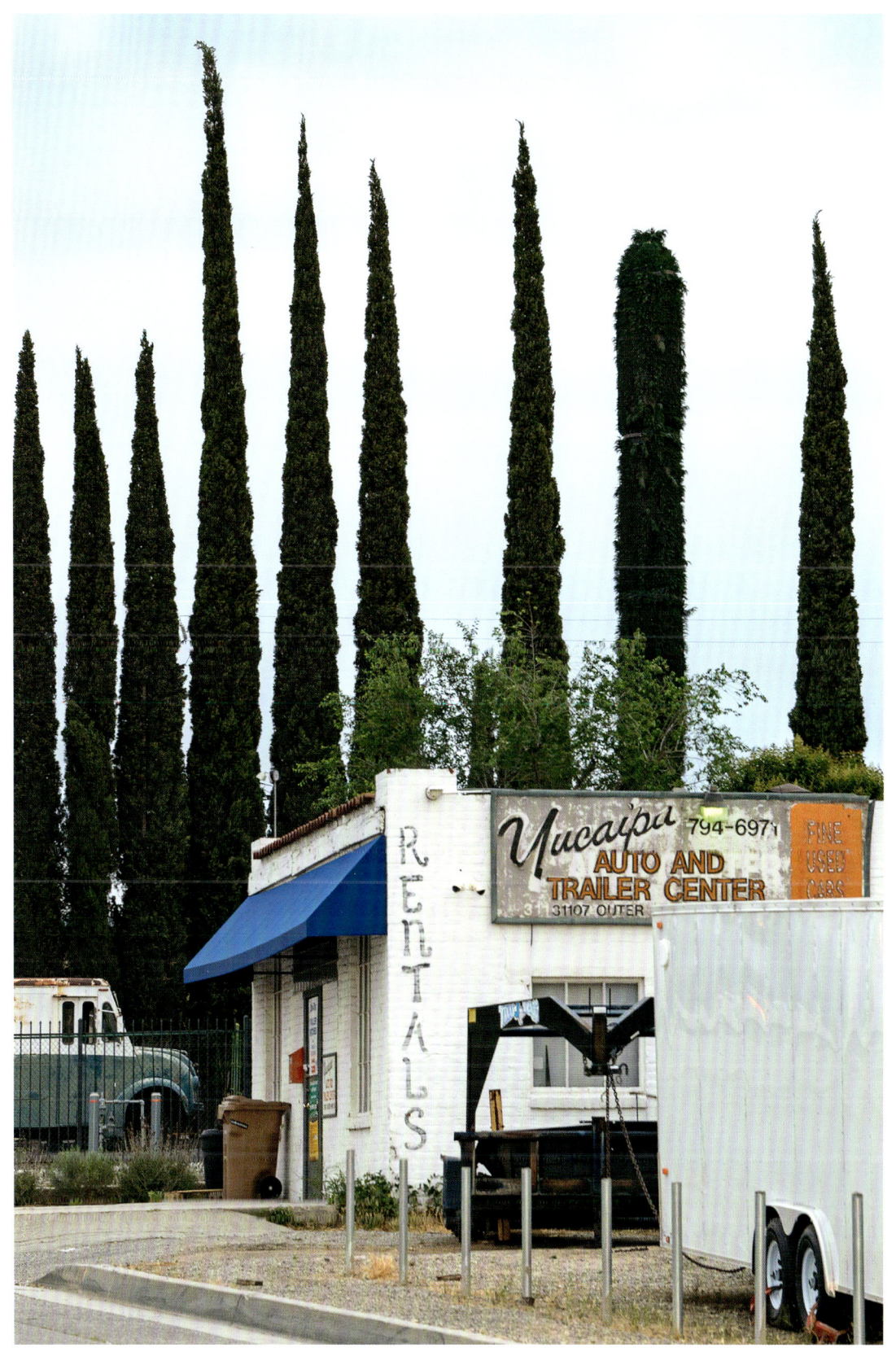

Italian Cypress, Yucaipa, CA – 2017

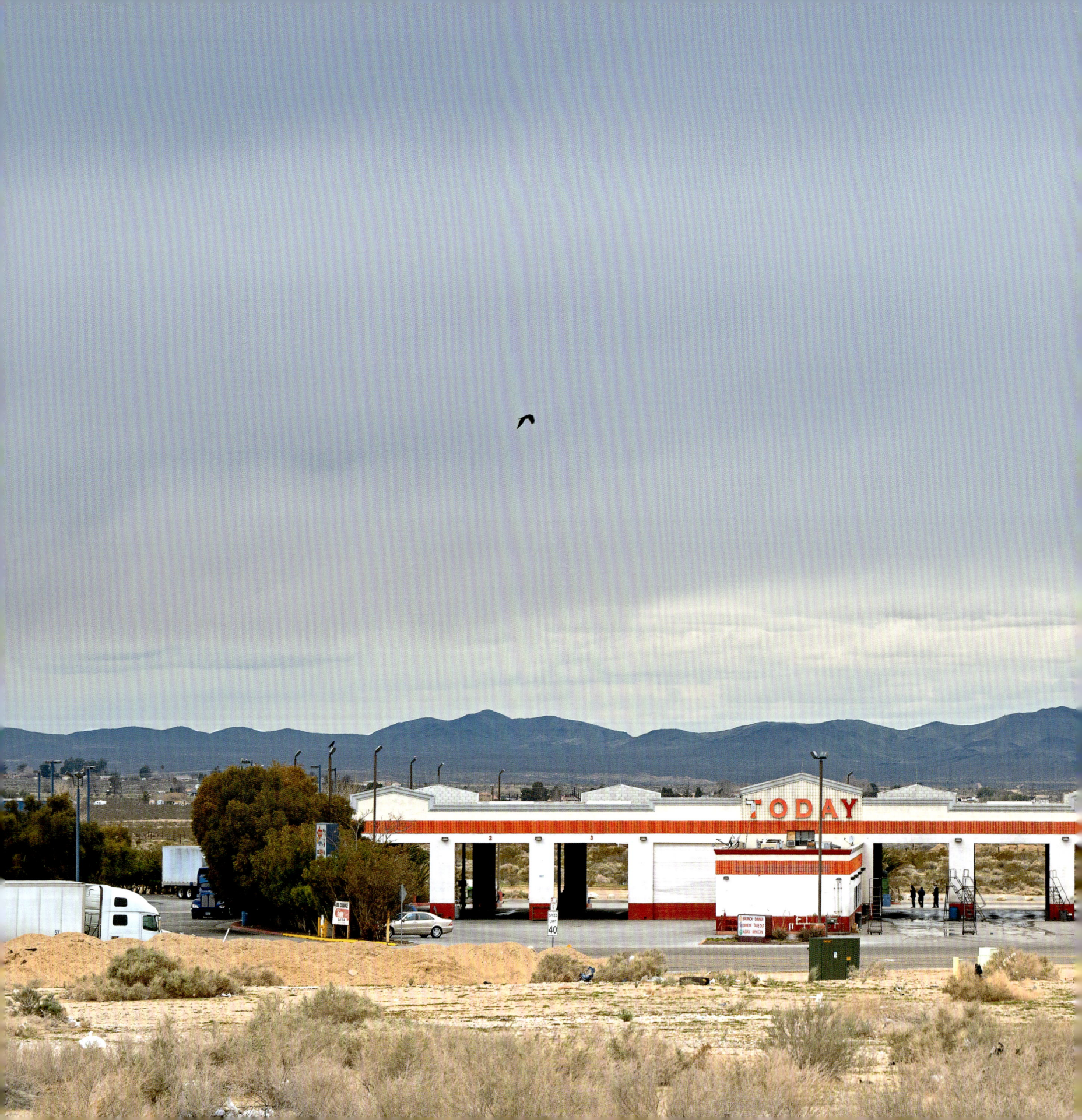

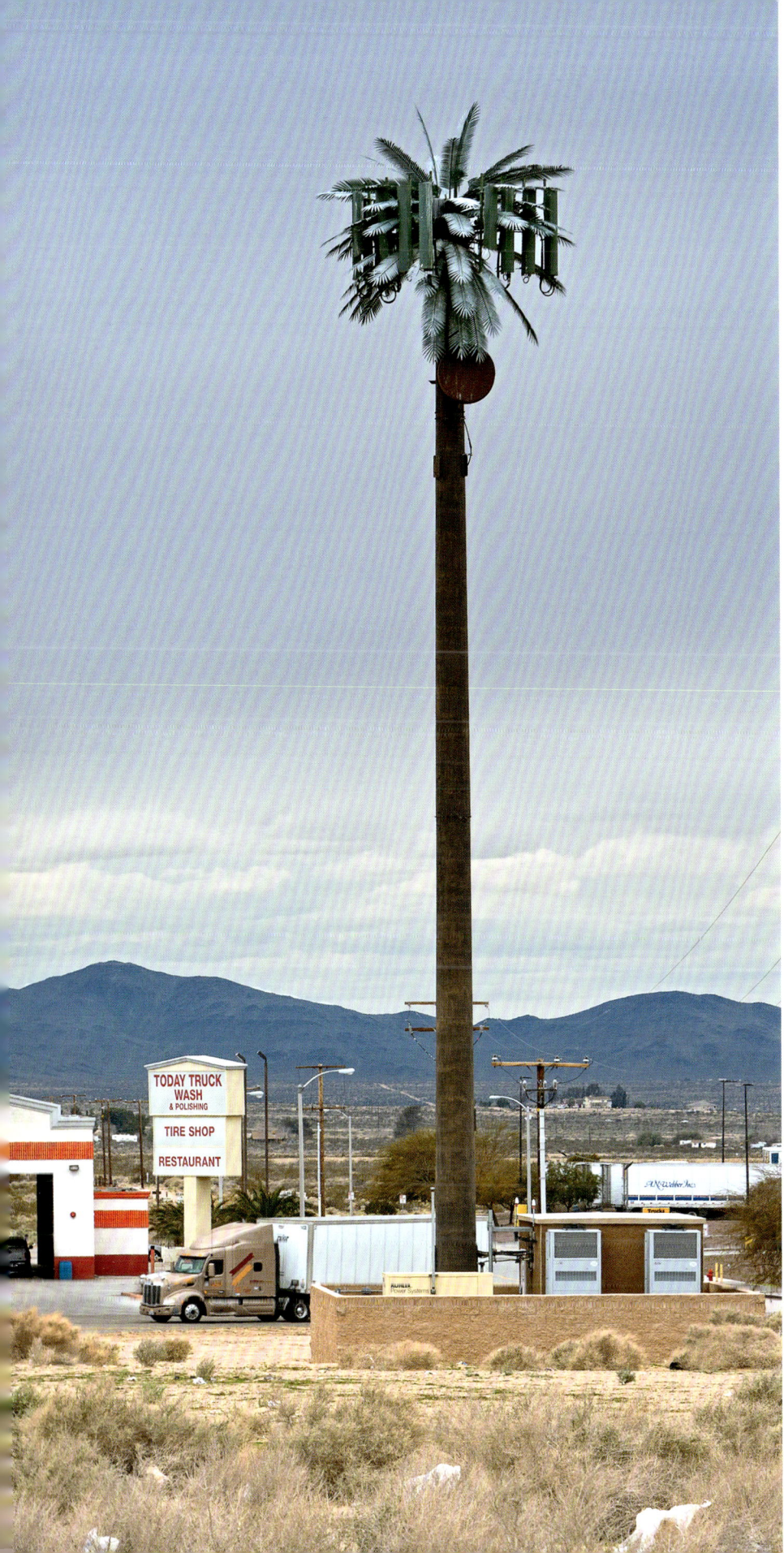

Current Situation, Barstow, CA – 2019

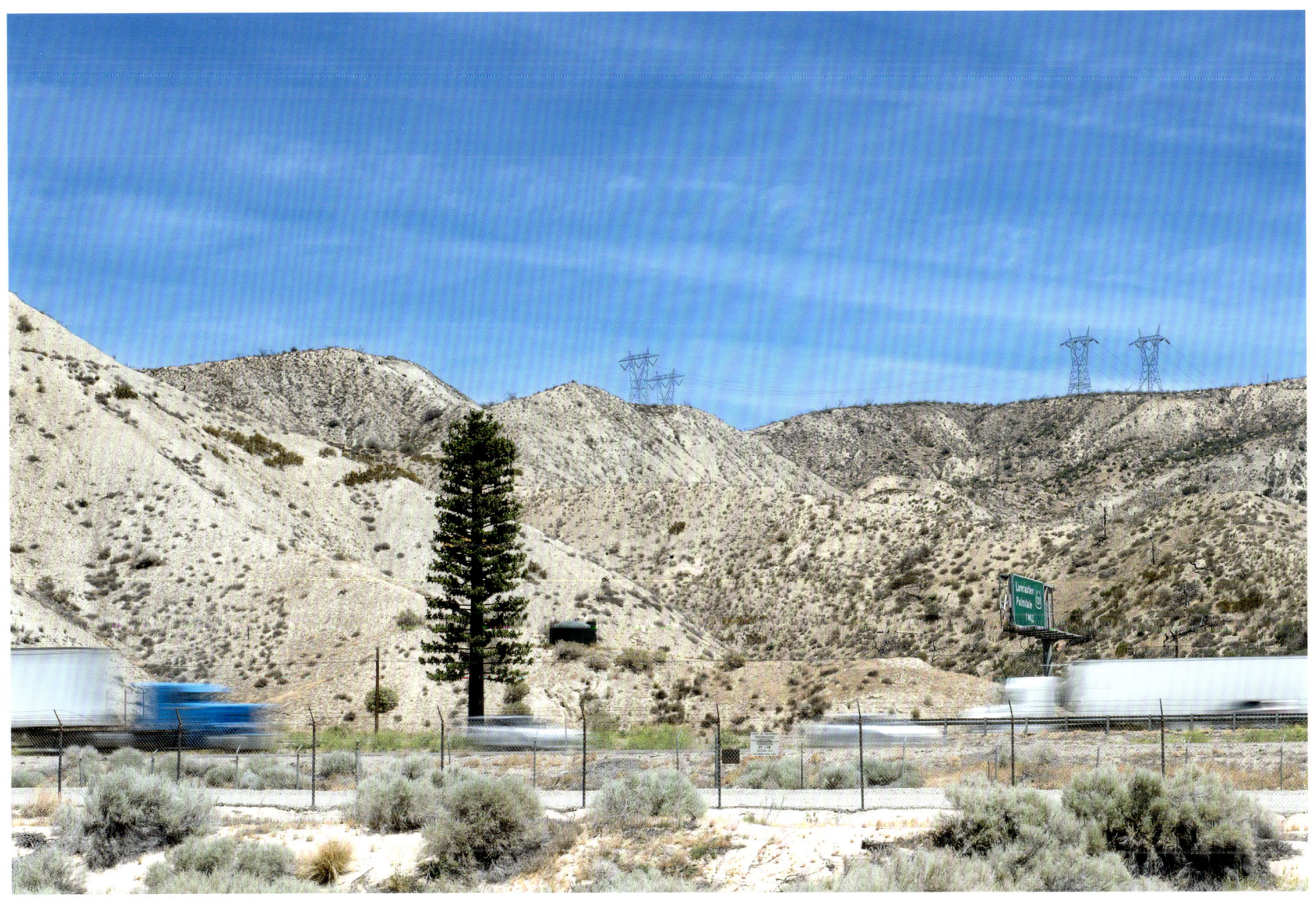

The Grapevine, Gorman, CA – 2017

WHAT'S UP WITH THAT TREE?

by Annette LeMay Burke

I first noticed a cell tower disguised as a tree in the early 2000s. Even living in the heart of Silicon Valley and surrounded by technology and its infrastructure, this tree felt out of place. For me, the fake foliage of trees such as these drew more attention to itself than it provided camouflage. While I was initially drawn to the towers' whimsical appearances, the more I photographed them, the more disconcerted I felt that technology was clandestinely modifying our environment. Would our children soon accept these towers as normal? I began to explore how this manufactured nature had imposed a contrived aesthetic in our neighborhoods. My photographs expose the towers' idiosyncratic disguises, highlight the variety of forms, and show how ubiquitous they are in our daily lives. Since the towers were mostly fake trees, I dubbed the series *Fauxliage*.

Cell phone towers are now entrenched as part of our built world. I began investigating why they are treated differently than other utility structures. Unlike power and landline phone companies, cellular service providers do not have eminent domain for their tower placement. They have to pay property owners to erect towers on their land. In an attempt to dampen the visual pollution and appease the neighbors, many early towers were disguised as trees. Today, as our insatiable demand for cellular service is ever increasing, the peculiar disguises have continued to proliferate as well. Primitive evergreens and palms have evolved into more sophisticated flagpoles, crosses, water towers, and cacti.

It is alright to decorate construction, but never construct decoration.
—Augustus Welby Northmore Pugin, architect of Big Ben

While we tolerate these curious poles so we can get five bars of service, perhaps Venturi, Brown, and Izenour's seminal 1972 architecture book, *Learning from Las Vegas*, offers some other clues to their acceptance. They observed how the American West's urban landscape and architecture was based on automobiles and the freeway, with an emphasis on vernacular commercial architecture. Las Vegas casinos, with their attention-grabbing neon signs and vast parking lots, certainly support this assessment. The authors proposed that this type of architecture was worthy of attention and praise. Disguised cell phone towers are definitely classified as commercial vernacular and I choose to observe them in that vein with my photos. Their camouflage works especially well when driving by at freeway speeds.

Perhaps our car culture is why the disguised towers are so prolific in the West, specifically the Southwest. Their appearance is now an inescapable part of the iconic western road trip and a familiar sight in the eight states that I visited for this project. In many meta moments, I was exchanging location data from the very tower I was searching for on my phone's map app.

Those are the best trees that combine use with ornament.
—John Evelyn, seventeenth-century English writer and gardener

I found many towers for this project by scanning the horizon while driving. Additionally, I always asked the locals for the strangest one in town. I researched the towers on the internet, scouring wayfaring sites and determining potential photo vantage points on Google Maps and Street View. The masquerading towers are often found shoehorned between freeways and frontage

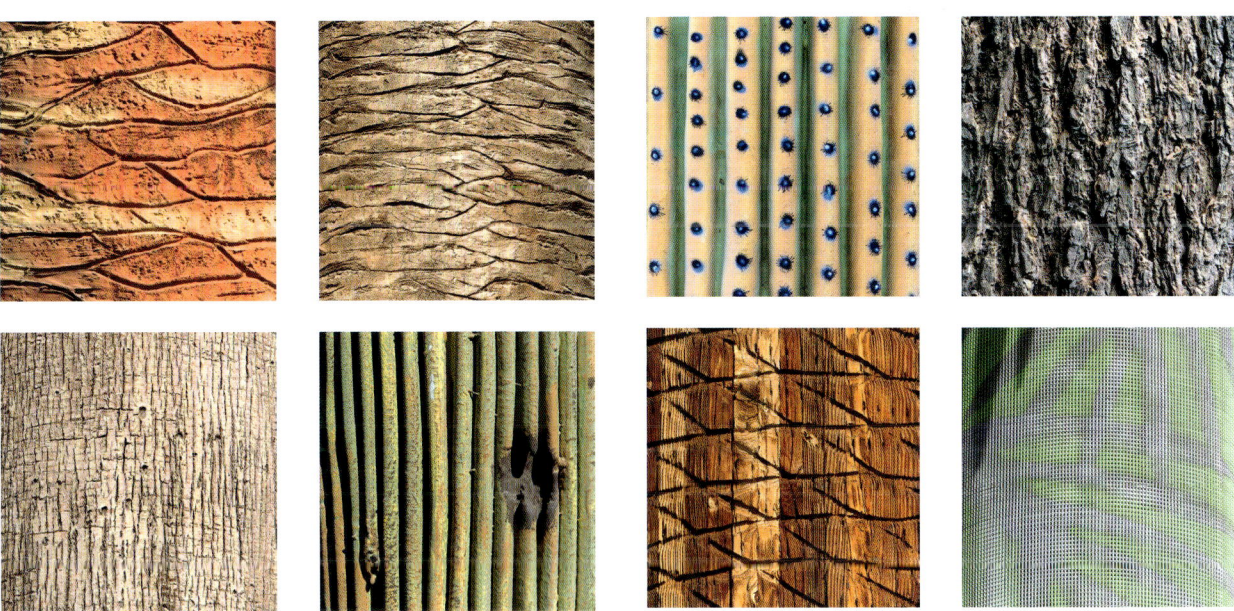

roads, tucked into suburbia and industrial areas, in mountain forests and the wide-open desert. Churches, schools, retail parking lots, self-storage units, and government buildings are common haunts. While I never saw a bird nest in a tower, my camera captured turkey vultures, falcons, red-winged blackbirds, seagulls, Hawaiian Nēnēs, and one peacock amongst the counterfeit trees. I also found horses, pit bulls, a Doberman, a cat, and one steel bison.

While the quirky disguises can be entertaining to look at, the towers present privacy and environmental concerns. The often-farcical pole disguises belie the equipment's covert ability to collect all the personal data transmitted from our cell phones. Our social media interactions, advertising clicks, location tracking pings, audio recordings by the always-listening Siri and Alexis, are all commoditized, sold, and stored by Big Tech and the government. Surveillance capitalism, especially perfecting the algorithms that can predict our behavior to advertisers, is big business in the twenty-first century.

The internet is the most liberating tool for humanity ever invented, and also the best for surveillance. It's not one or the other. It's both.
—John Perry Barlow, co-founder of the Electronic Freedom Frontier

The Patriot Act's sweeping powers and its myriad of "sunsets," extensions, and reauthorizations make it unclear when or if the NSA is collecting your sensitive personal data and phone calls. In 2020, the US government bought cell phone location information from commercial data brokers for use by ICE, the IRS, the CDC, and the Secret Service. This practice allows law enforcement agents to bypass obtaining a warrant. When thought of in this context, the kitschy tower costumes seem more nefarious.

In addition to the visual disruption of the landscape by these corporate masts, the plastic leaves that fall off the imitation trees are impacting the environment as well. The leaves drop off due to weather and aging. They litter the surrounding area and small pieces can easily enter the ecosystem. The trees are truly aesthetically unappealing at this point and are often refurbished with new branches and fresh leaves. I collected many fallen "botanical samples" from the ground beneath the trees and used them to create UV cyanotype prints—a process that English botanist Anna Atkins pioneered with algae in the 1800s. (She was also the first person to illustrate a book with photographic images.) As I was washing the leaves and preparing to create the photograms in the sun, many of the thin, timeworn evergreen needles were breaking apart into tiny pieces and spreading throughout my backyard. I then realized that what had started as an attempt to reduce visual pollution was now creating plastic pollution.

Cellular technology has become an indispensable part of our modern lives. The fifth generation (5G) of cellular technology will be a leap forward in its evolution. With near instantaneous latency and greater bandwidth, it will allow for self-driving vehicles, real-time remote interactions—such as robotic surgery and virtual reality, smarter internet of things, and home broadband. The rollout of 5G will bring changes to the cell tower terrain too. 5G utilizes smaller equipment that is easier to hide— think small antennas integrated into the tops of streetlight poles. Due to changing technology and the public's increased visual tolerance, elaborately disguised "fauxliage" towers could start disappearing and be considered an anachronism of the early twenty-first century. The decorated towers could join drive-up photo kiosks, phone booths, newsstands, and drive-in movie theaters as architectural relics of the past.

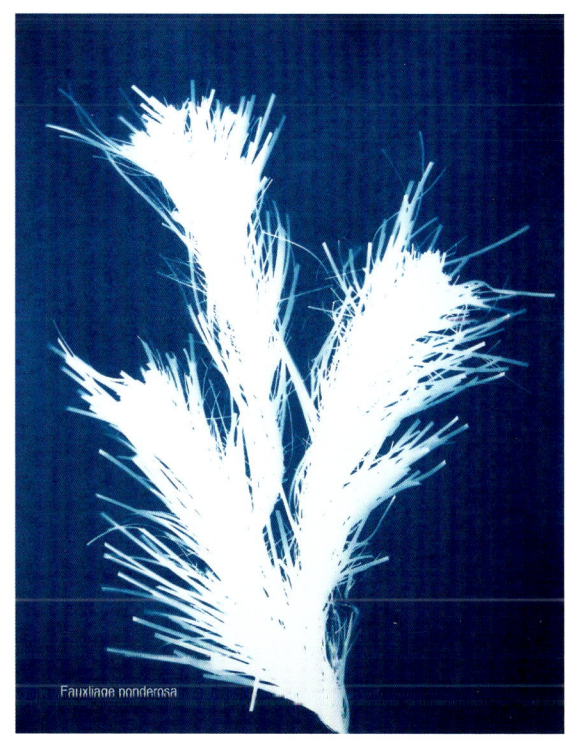

Fauxliage ponderosa

Under observation, we act less free, which means we effectively are less free.
—Edward Snowden, former NSA Analyst

Annette LeMay Burke is an award-winning photographic artist and Northern California native who lives in the heart of Silicon Valley. She is a longtime observer of the western landscape and how it has changed over time. Her work has been exhibited throughout the United States and in Europe. For further information, see: www.atelierlemay.com.

ACKNOWLEDGMENTS

The support and encouragement of my husband, Martin, and our son, Colin, has been an integral part of my photography practice. Creating some of these photos was a joint adventure with Martin, especially on our RV escapades in the Southwest. I always appreciate his patience and understanding when I spot a great potential image and we need to "pull the car over now." Colin's kindred critical eye is always helpful in the editing process.

A special thanks to my parents, John and Joanne, who both passed away within a few months of each other while I was creating this body of work. Their dedication and implicit acceptance of a creative, crafty, and often-quirky life made this project seem possible and normal. Plus, years of family road trips set me up for success with this particular endeavor.

A big thank you to master photographer Arthur Meyerson, who has been a mentor to me, especially in the early phases of this project. His inspiration and reassurance drove me forward with this work.

I was greatly influenced by the late Brian Tramontana's thoughtful critique and backing of my work when I first started studying photography. I am also grateful for the collective he created, Maverick Photographers. My fellow photographers in this group have provided years of valuable discourse, encouragement, and friendship.

The esteemed Ann M. Jastrab has been a champion of my work since I first met her. I am indebted to her once again for writing the foreword to this book.

Thank you all!